DARRYL STINGLEY:

Happy to be Alive

DARRYL STINGLEY:

Happy to be Alive

Darryl Stingley
with Mark Mulvoy

BEAUFORT BOOKS, INC.

New York / Toronto

Library of Congress Cataloging in Publication Data

Stingley, Darryl.
Darryl Stingley: happy to be alive.

1. Stingley, Darryl.   2. Football players—United States—Biography.
3. Quadriplegics—United States—Biography.   I. Mulvoy, Mark.   II. Title.
GV939.S745A33   1983   796.332′092′4 [B]   83-7135
ISBN 0-8253-0157-2

Published in the United States by Beaufort Books, Inc., New York.
Published simultaneously in Canada by General Publishing Co. Limited

Designer: Ellen Lo Giudice
Printed in the U.S.A.   First Edition
10 9 8 7 6 5 4 3 2 1

Acknowledgments

In my thirty-two years of life, I have learned many things—to say the least. Probably the most significant and important phases of my life, which I've tried to recount in this book, were influenced by the people I mention here. It is my sincerest belief that had not all of these people, in some point in time, passed through my life, it would not have been the same; nor would I have been what I consider the luckiest and most blessed individual on this planet Earth.

First and foremost, a very special thanks goes to God, our Heavenly Father and Creator of all things, for making me what I am and what I will eventually become.

To my parents, Harold and Hilda Stingley; to my brothers, Wayne and Harold, Jr.; and to my sister, Andrea—the most important people in my life who collectively, with their guidance, helped shape and mold the "me" the world has come to know—I love you all.

To Martine, the mother of my children; to Darryl Jr. and Derek, for your never ending love.

To all my relatives—cousins, aunts, uncles, nephews, nieces and in-laws, you, too, have made a difference.

Otis and Yvonne Armstrong, thanks for your love, and for being my spiritual advisors; Dr. Pont and the staff of Eden Hospital, Castro Valley, California; Dr. Vinod Saghal, Rehabilitation Institute of Chicago; Sports Advisors Group: Jack Sands, Steve Freyer, Sandy Weedon, Emily Stein—for being more than advisors, for being friends and family, thanks for your love, I love you back; Samuel Cunningham, Jr., for being a big brother to me; Ron Echols and Harry Watkins, good friends who passed on but left me a lot; Darryl Williams, the strongest teenager I know; Mrs. Simmons, for holding on and being strong; Kenny Hudson; Claudia Smith, you are everything, I love you; Nick Seabrook, my first mentor; Barbara J. Bradford; Dave Luke; Cleve Washington; Flossie Brown, for your good cooking which gave me much strength to endure; Byron "Pee Wee" Mitchell; Cheryl D. Gouldsby, for being my left arm, I love you; Louis Price and family; Fred and Ken Williams and family; Tevis Luckett; Alton Hardaway; Joe Wilson; Joe Hudson; Leona Pasqualetti; Malcolm Hemphill, Jr. and family; Jim Peoples; Ben Ward; Luther Bedford and family; Thelma Nelson, your flowers bring beauty in life; Bob and Norris Young; Big Boy, Betty and Lynne Mendes, my family away from home; John Madden and family; William Sullivan, Jr. and family; Entire Patriots Organization; Members of '73–'78 Patriots; Tony McGee and family; Shelby Jordan and family; Stanley Morgan and family; Russ Francis; Leon Gray and family; Prentice McCray; Coach Chuck Fairbanks and family; Toby Fairbanks; George S. Halas and Chicago Bears; George H. Allen and Chicago Blitz; Coach Ray Perkins; Coach Raymond Berry; Pinkey Newell; Doc Holmes; Mrs. Dale Richey; Mrs. Rosemary Blakesley; Jim Karas; Judy Ranka; John Bellamy; the workers at Rehabilitation Institute of Chicago, who do so much for so many; Stevie Wonder, a true inspiration; Marvin Gaye; Muhammad Ali, thanks for one of the "greatest" experiences in my life; Della Reese; Al Jarreau; Dick Gregory, a true "Brother"; Gil Scott-Heron; Congressman Walter Fauntroy; Vice President George Bush; Howard Cosell, for showing me your sincerity; Mike Douglas; Senator Edward Kennedy; Mayor Harold Washington, for being my hero; Reverend Jesse Jackson; Mother Ford, living proof of what faith can do; Good Hope Church of God in Christ, Chicago, for their continued prayers; John H. Johnson and Johnson Publications; Lacy Gray, for the sunshine in your smile; Richard A. Sugar; Abe Thompson; Dianne Thompson; Ernie Kramer; Carl Sissacs; Cleve Walker; The City of Chicago; The City of Boston; Chicago Media; Boston Media; United States Jaycees; Chicago Bulls, White Sox, Cubs; Mark Mulvoy and Tom Woll, for helping me recount these events of my life; Glenn Franklin, I owe you my fourth life, smiles; to all the groups and organizations who saw reason to honor me; because to honor me is to give praise to the Glory of God; and all of this is inspiring.

To countless others that I failed to mention—you know who you are. Because God has allowed me to know all of you in my lifetime, my life has been enriched far beyond what an average existence can anticipate. It is my belief that my cup runneth over with the love and affection that I have received from others. Because of this, I often feel guilty that I have not given as much as I have received. Therefore, it is my wish that by writing this book, and exposing some of my innermost thoughts, feelings, and personal situations, it has given you all a part of me; and if there is such a thing, "the debt has been paid."

Peace and love and may God bless each of you as He has continued to bless me.

To the memory of Melinda Embry,
Mama Babe, my great-great grandmother,
a tower of strength whose spirit is ever present.

Contents

1 · Am I Gonna Be All Right?

Darryl Stingley last evening suffered a fractured dislocation injury of his cervical spine. Neurosurgeon Dr. Manard
Pont was assisted by Dr. Donald Fink, the Oakland Raiders' team physician, in an operation that lasted approx-
imately one hour. Stingley had cervical-traction tongs
placed with the correction of the dislocation. This morning
he has gained some right-arm motion and has some sensation in his entire body. There is NO PROGNOSIS at this
time. No photos. No interviews. No visitors.
—Medical Bulletin No. 1, 9:00 A.M. PDT, Sunday, August
13, 1978

The thing I hated most about life as a player in the National
Football League was the time spent in training camp. It's a
necessary evil. If anybody says he likes training camp, he's lying.
The only people who ever say nice things about it are the rookies,
and they don't know any better. They're just trying to impress all
the coaches with their gung ho attitude, so they won't get a

13

one-way ticket back home when NFL rosters are reduced to regular-season limits.

It was a typically hot and steamy day in mid-July 1978 when I drove onto the campus of Bryant College in North Smithfield, Rhode Island, and officially checked into the New England Patriots' training camp. I was a five-year veteran, coming off my best season as a wide receiver—thirty-nine catches for 657 yards and five touchdowns—and, well, I wasn't really worried about having to win a job. The way I saw it, I was a shoo-in. Head coach Chuck Fairbanks and receivers coach Raymond Berry had as much as told me that during the off-season. Also, the Patriots and my lawyer-agent, Jack Sands, were wrapping up negotiations on my new contract, a deal that would pay me more than $500,000 over five years and put me into a salary league with Lynn Swann of the Pittsburgh Steelers and Harold Jackson of the Los Angeles Rams, the highest-paid receivers in the NFL.

Still, I had worked out every day at home in Chicago from early February until early July, when I left to drive to camp, and I was in the best shape I'd ever been. My goals for '78 were Super Bowl for the Patriots and All-Pro for Darryl Stingley, Number 84.

Sure enough, the first three weeks of camp were as boring as ever. It was the same thing each and every day: up at 7:00 A.M., breakfast, practice in full pads from 9:00 to 11:00, lunch, nap, meetings to study film or be shown new plays, practice again from 3:00 to 5:00, dinner at 6:30, meetings again from 8:00 to 10:00, lights out at 11:00 P.M. You didn't dare miss curfew, either; the fine for violators was $500, no questions asked.

Finally, after three weeks of beating on one another in one-on-one drills, running pass patterns against teammates and knocking down blocking dummies at Bryant College, we were ready for the four-game exhibition season. And in 1978, the NFL schedule maker was good to us.

Our first exhibition was Saturday night, August 5, against the

14

Rams in Los Angeles: our second was Saturday night, August 12, against the Raiders at Oakland. Normally, NFL teams return home immediately after a game, flying through the night if necessary, but our coaches didn't think it made much sense to fly to Los Angeles, stay there for thirty-six hours, fly back to Boston, practice for a few days, return to California, stay in Oakland for thirty-six hours and then fly all the way back to Boston. The way they figured it, we'd suffer jet lag and be all worn out before the regular season even started.

So, after playing, and beating, the Rams in L.A., we flew north to San Francisco and set up training camp for a week at St. Mary's College in the Bay Area. Everyone agreed that it was the best week of camp we had ever experienced. Oh, we had curfew, meetings and some mandatory meals at St. Mary's, but we also had plenty of time to tour around San Francisco. The nearest city to Bryant College is Providence, and Providence sure isn't San Francisco.

Two nights before the game against the Raiders, Prentice McCray, one of our defensive backs, and I were having a couple of beers, when I told him that I'd been feeling strong negative vibes, really strong, stronger than any I'd had before. I'm not psychic or anything, but, as I told Prentice, it was as if there were a little bird sitting on my shoulder saying, "Hey, man, something's going to happen to you, something bad, really bad."

Prentice told me not to think about it, but I kept looking for that something to happen. I didn't know what it would be, but I didn't think it would be related to football. Maybe I was going to get food poisoning from some bad Fisherman's Wharf fish, or maybe I was going to be traded to some other team. Maybe . . . maybe . . . maybe. I couldn't get all those negative vibes out of my mind. And they were still with me as we bussed over to the Oakland-Alameda County Coliseum Saturday to play the Raiders.

Crossing the Bay Bridge, I began to think about the Raiders and some of their players. A New England–Oakland game, even in the preseason, would not be just another NFL game. It would be a war. We hated the Raiders because of the way they played the game; football players may talk macho, but football players don't like cheap-shot artists—those in my opinion, who always hit you a little harder than necessary and purposefully aim for more vulnerable parts of the body—and the Oakland roster was filled with them.

More than any other NFL team, the Raiders thrived on a game of intimidation. When I lined up against an Oakland player, I could expect him to say something derogatory to me about my mother or my father or my ancestors or my sexual preference. Or maybe he'd criticize my ability. Or he'd question my courage. You name it, the Raiders did it. Anything to agitate. And when it came to blocking and tackling, the Raiders always operated on the no-holds-barred theory. Anything went with Oakland.

Approaching the stadium I remembered the way George Atkinson, one of the Oakland safeties, had clotheslined Russ Francis, our tight end, in the 1976 playoffs and, as I recall, busted his nose. It was a perfect example of what I'd come to expect from the Raiders.

In fact, I'd had my own problems with Atkinson in that game. On the very first play of the game I went into motion, running from my wide-out position back toward the formation, and turned upfield to block their strong safety—Atkinson. We were running a sweep. As I blocked Atkinson, I suddenly saw his elbow coming directly at my head. It was a rude awakening. I turned my head away at the last minute, but he got me in the chest. The blow was so devastating, it felt like he had a brick attached to his arm.

"It's gonna be like that all day, you bleeper," Atkinson said to me.

And it was. On another series, the Raiders gang-tackled me down near their goal line and hit me so hard—and in so many places—that I didn't know where I was. I got up, but I was really dazed. I just looked for the white uniforms and started to walk away. I was on Queer Street.

"Darryl," I said to myself as our bus reached the stadium that evening in August '78, "it could be another long night."

As always, I was nervous sitting in the dressing room reviewing my assignments for the game. Little Toby Fairbanks, the coach's son, was at my side, as always, and helped me put on my uniform. I was still feeling uncomfortable, but about what I didn't know. Deep inside me I had so many strong negative vibes—the kind I'd talked to Prentice about during the week—that I had trouble focusing my mind on the game. Finally, we went onto the field for the kickoff; I was the last player out.

Once on the field, I started to break into a trot, looked down, and saw I had forgotten to take my watch off. I remembered that I had done the same thing before our game at Oakland the year before. The fact is, you don't play football wearing a watch. What had I been thinking about? I couldn't go back to the locker room to leave the watch there, since it was too close to kickoff. So I went over to Toby, gave the watch to him, and asked him to keep it for me until the end of the game.

Our coaching staff had decided to play the regular starting offense for at least the first half and then experiment with rookies and free agents in the second, so I was on the field at the start.

Early in the game, Steve Grogan, our quarterback, called a play in which I was to run a D pattern, a down-and-in route, as a decoy. The ball was snapped, I ran my route, and as I cut into the middle, I looked to see what the Oakland defense was doing. I should've known. It was number 32 of the Raiders making a beeline for me. Thirty-two was Jack Tatum, the Oakland free safety, a player whose total approach to football was, in my opinion, even more vicious than George Atkinson's.

I couldn't understand why Tatum was even in the neighbor-hood where I was running. His responsibility on the play was to cover not the short middle, where I was, but the deep middle—

17

that is, everything deeper than about 15 yards from the line of scrimmage. No Patriot was supposed to get behind Tatum on this play.

But Tatum was so intent on zeroing in on me—so he could clock me if Grogan threw the ball to me—that he left the deep middle open. The play was designed to go long, not short, and Stanley Morgan, our wide receiver who lined up on the opposite side of the field from me, broke free into the area where Tatum should have been, caught Grogan's pass and scored a long, and unbelievably easy, touchdown.

"Tough luck, Tatum," I thought as I saw Stanley cruise toward the end zone with not a Raider in sight. Tatum never got me on the play, and we burned him for a touchdown.

Perfect.

The game moved along, and Oakland led by a field goal as we approached the half. We were on a long drive, gaining good yardage on practically every play, when Grogan called my favorite play: the end-around, or reverse, with me carrying the ball. I'd had great success with the reverse in previous games against Oakland; when we beat the Raiders 48–17 in 1976, I caught two passes for touchdowns and twice ran reverses for long gains that brought us near their goal line.

Once again I broke the reverse for big yardage. I gained 24 yards but must have run 50, cutting up, cutting in, cutting back to dodge hits from Tatum and all those other cats swinging their heavily padded arms. The play ended when I stepped out of bounds. I was tired and winded. It was only a preseason game, a meaningless exhibition, and I was thinking, "Hey, Coach, get some rookies in here and give me a rest." I mean, I was coming off my best season, and the coaches all knew what I could do. So, what did I have to prove to them, or to anyone else? I tried to come off the field to catch my breath, just for a play, but as I was running toward the sideline, everyone was waving at me, shouting for me to get back to the huddle. So back I went. I was still tired two plays later, when we had a third down and 8 yards to go for the first down at the Oakland 24-yard line.

Ron Erhardt, our offensive coordinator, was watching the game from his usual spot in a private glass-enclosed room in the press box, high above the field. He wore a headset connected to Fairbanks's headset down on the sidelines, and laid out before him was our game plan for the Raiders. Erhardt's—we called Ron Fargo because he had been the head coach at North Dakota State University—major assignment during a game was to assess each New England offensive situation with respect to down, distance, and the expected Oakland defensive strategy and then relay a suggested play to Fairbanks, who in turn would messenger that play, or maybe one of his own choosing, to Grogan via one of our other players. The quarterback didn't get to call too many plays under the Fairbanks system.

Standing in the huddle, waiting for the play to arrive from the bench, I thought to myself that we had three basic options: 1) We could go for broke and try a 24-yard pass for a touchdown; 2) we could try some type of pass play or even a running play to pick up the 8 yards needed for a first down, thus prolonging the drive; or 3) we could move the ball safely into position for a 35- to 40-yard field-goal attempt, a chip shot for our placekicker, John Smith.

The play arrived, and suddenly I heard Grogan call out: "Ninety-four Slant." I wasn't surprised. All week long at St. Mary's we had worked on the 94 Slant, an old play in Fairbanks's repertoire but one we hadn't used in training camp or in the exhibition game against the Rams the week before. It was a good play for Grogan, or any quarterback, because it offered him a variety of options.

My assignment on the 94 Slant was to run an 8-yard slant-in pattern; that is, I was to line up strong side right—the strong side always being the side of the quarterback on which the tight end lines up—and then go downfield for 8 yards and turn into the middle of the field at about a 45-degree angle. At that point I would be between the linebackers and the cornerback—an open target for a second or two.

Grogan could throw the ball to me. He could throw it to the weak-side wide receiver, Stanley Morgan, who would be slanting in at a wider angle from left to right—I'd be slanting in from right to left—slightly deeper down the field. He could throw to the tight end, Francis, who would be running a short diagonal pattern toward the right sideline. He could dump the ball off to one of his running backs. Or, if everything was covered, he could run the ball himself, which is something Grogan always liked to do. The key thing was, the 94 Slant had to be a quick pass. Grogan had to take the ball from center, drop back one-two-three steps, then throw the ball to a spot. Within that time he had to study his options, find the open man, then make the pass work.

It was a tough play for Grogan to make because he was basically a running, roll-out quarterback, not the pure dropback passer from the Johnny Unitas school. Grogan worked long and hard with the coaches on his dropback technique, but he was never really comfortable back there in the pocket.

Grogan's major flaw as a quarterback was his tendency to force a pass to a primary receiver who was well covered, rather than throw it to a more open secondary target. In practice the coaches were always onto Grogan not to commit himself so completely to the primary receiver, to look away from that man and throw the ball to a secondary receiver who was in the clear. In fact, at one of our meetings after practice at St. Mary's, two of the assistant coaches, John Polonchek, who handled the quarterbacks, and Raymond Berry, who handled the receivers, told Grogan that whenever we called the 94 Slant, the weak side would probably always be open. "Check out Stanley Morgan slanting in deep on the Ninety-four Slant," they told him. "Don't commit yourself to Darryl or to Russ."

It made sense. Russ and I would be working the 94 Slant on a combo pattern from the strong, in this case the right, side of the field. The strongside linebacker would be working against Russ, while the strongside cornerback would be working against me. The strongside safety would be there, too. Meanwhile, on the weak, or left, side, Stanley Morgan would most likely get no more than single coverage. And, well, there weren't too many defensive backs who could cover Stanley Morgan one-on-one.

So, we broke out of the huddle and lined up in the 94 Slant. Grogan called his signals, the ball was snapped—and the play was on.

Free safeties are trained to read the quarterback's head and eyes and react accordingly. Jack Tatum was the Oakland free safety, and he obviously had no trouble reading Grogan on this play: from the snap of the ball to his set-up to his release of the pass, Steve looked in one direction and one direction only. He never tried to steer Tatum off the intended target by glancing at Stanley Morgan . . . or by looking at Russ Francis . . . or by faking a short flip to one of his running backs. Jack Tatum didn't have to be a genius to know that Steve Grogan would be throwing the football to only one person.

Me.

If Grogan had scanned the field, he would have noticed that Russ had encountered some problems while running his short down-and-out pattern and suddenly was too close to me, making the area far too congested; and also that Stanley had broken clear down the left side and was as open as he could be, with not a Raider in sight. A pass to Stanley would have meant a touchdown.

But Steve never looked at Russ Francis or Stanley Morgan. He looked only at me.

To make matters even worse, not only had Grogan failed to check out his options, but he also held on to the ball too long. As a result, when I broke toward the middle of the field in front of Raider cornerback Lester Hayes and was ready to catch the ball, it wasn't there. I knew at that moment that the play was dead. The ball had to be waiting for me when I made my break—when I

21

planted my foot and turned in—or else the area would be jammed up with defensive players when it finally arrived.

At last—maybe a second or a second and a half late—there was the ball . . . well over my head. We had a drill in training camp where one of the coaches would throw the ball over our head and we had to leap for the grab. We were trained to adjust to the ball, to get it at whatever cost. We were supposed to be ball hawks. And my desire to catch anything thrown near me made me want to adjust, to spring into the air and make the play. Hey, the Patriots weren't giving me a rich new contract because I didn't make the tough catches. They were paying me big bucks—or were about to—to catch everything thrown my way. That was my job.

I never had a chance to catch this pass, though. The ball just flew past my outstretched fingertips as I leaped as high into the air as I could. The ball was so close I could feel it going by. I was coming back to earth, and what did I see, suddenly, in a flash—I can still see it now, plain as day; I'll never forget it—Jack Tatum, Number 32, barreling toward me.

I felt as though I was suspended in mid air, a feather succumbing ever so slowly to the pull of gravity, and here was this monster train coming at me full steam. I was looking Tatum dead in the eye and saw his look. His eyes and face were on fire. He was cocking his bone, as we call it, his forearm. And he was coming fast. He was 210 pounds. I saw him—saw the bone coming—and dropped my head to get it as low as possible so I could duck the bone. But it was too late. He delivered the blow. He cracked me on the head and on the back of my neck with full force.

I hit the ground with a thud and tried to get up, as I had so many times before, but I couldn't move. I felt like I was the cornerstone of a high-rise building, as if an elephant had his foot on my chest. I wasn't in pain, or at least I couldn't feel any. I just couldn't move. Not a muscle. Nothing. I couldn't feel my feet. Or my arms. Or my body. I couldn't feel anything. Everything inside my body was saying, "Get up, Darryl," but I couldn't move.

God, we were down around the 20-yard line, and I loved it there. That was Touchdown Territory, the place where I got a chance to work my little moves, to get free, to catch touchdown passes. I wanted to get back to the huddle for the next play.

In the press box Ron Erhardt said to one of the other Patriot coaches, "Darryl looks like he sure got his bell rung."

Almost immediately, while I was trying to move various parts of my body, Tom Healion, our trainer, appeared at my side. Tom normally didn't come onto the field to see an injured player until one of the officials gave him a signal, but the instant I got hit he ran onto the field. When he got there, I was lying on my left side. "Tom, am I gonna be all right? Am I gonna be all right? Am I gonna—"

"Sure, sure, everything'll be fine, Buddy," Tom kept saying. "Don't you worry. . . . Don't you worry one bit. . . . You're gonna be okay, Buddy . . ." Tom reached down and held my right hand.

"Darryl, squeeze my hand," he said. Usually, if a player can squeeze that hand, the trainer will say, "Let me see you move your foot." I couldn't squeeze Tom's hand. He never asked me to move my foot. And I was worried. God knows I was worried.

Tom waved to the sidelines, and Dr. A.V. Mariano, the Patriots' preseason team physician and a cardiovascular surgeon at Norwood Hospital outside Boston, ran onto the field. Tom tried to make me feel comfortable, but I kept asking him, "Tom, am I gonna be all right? Tom, am I gonna be all right?"—over and over and over.

He couldn't say, "No, Darryl, you're not." So he said to me over and over, "Darryl, don't you worry. We're gonna take care of you." He said it a dozen times, then another dozen.

When Dr. Mariano arrived at my side, he checked my reflexes, starting with my elbows, then my hands, then my knees, then my feet. Normally, if your knee is tapped in a certain spot, the nerve will respond and the leg will jump. It's a standard reflex test. He was looking for any movement, any reflex at all. I had none. I saw

Chuck Fairbanks looking down at me, but then he was gone.

Dr. Mariano tried my knees again. Nothing moved. Nothing. I knew what was happening, or what I thought was happening, and I was frightened. Suddenly, I was having a hard time breathing. My head had been put into makeshift traction, and the new position of my neck and head seemed to be affecting my breathing.

"Tom, Tom, Tom—I can't breathe."

"Darryl, you'll be fine, just relax and take some deep breaths."

When I said I was having trouble breathing, Dr. Mariano decided that he should remove my helmet. The two of them—Dr. Mariano and Tom Healion—now put my neck in a cervical-traction unit and got it into a position where they could take off the helmet. Immediately, I felt better and started to breathe more easily.

All this time, Tom was face to face with me, comforting me, telling me I wasn't alone, that he was with me. Dr. Mariano, Tom, and the emergency medical service staff on duty at the stadium delicately placed me on a stretcher, and I heard the roar of the crowd. I had heard that same roar many times before in Oakland, but never for someone on an opposing team. It warmed me up.

Suddenly I was being moved across the field. "Tom, Tom, will you go with me?"

"Darryl, I want to, but I can't leave. I've gotta stay with the club. Dr. Mariano is going with you, and the ambulance crew will be with you, and there'll be doctors waiting at the hospital. What you've got to do is relax, if you can. Take some deep breaths. You're gonna be O.K., Darryl."

They put my stretcher into the ambulance. Tom held my hand and told me again that I'd be O.K. and not to worry. Then he was gone, and we were off. Tom told me later that he went right to Coach Fairbanks and told him, "Coach, Darryl's got a very serious injury."

I was conscious but in shock on the ride from the stadium to Eden Hospital in nearby Castro Valley. The siren on the ambulance had a piercing tone, and we had a California Highway Patrol motorcycle escort all the way. As the ambulance sped along, one thing kept running through my mind: "What's wrong with me? Why can't I feel my arms? My legs? Why can't I move?" It was a totally new experience for me. I had always had remarkable command over my body. There was nothing of a physical nature that I ever felt incapable of doing. But now . . . now I couldn't move a thing. Why? God, tell me why?

We pulled up to the emergency entrance of the hospital, where dozens of people seemed to be waiting in their white coats; some looking, and others running frantically. It sure seemed to me that confusion had set in. Doctors were yelling to get this and get that. A nurse screamed, "Clear the way. Clear the way." They wheeled me out of the ambulance and down some corridors into the emergency room. The place was in an uproar.

A nurse appeared, and she had a big silver cutter in her hand. What the hell was that for? While I was wondering about it, she started cutting my shoes off. She started at the toe and worked straight up, nonstop. Off came my shoes and socks. Then she cut off my football pants and all the tape, piece by piece, inch by inch. It was like she was cutting me up into so many little morsels.

As she moved up my legs with her big silver cutter, I began to breathe heavier and heavier, faster and faster. The shock was becoming traumatic. And then she came to my chest and started to cut away my Patriots jersey with the big "84" on it. As she reached my stomach and began to move up my chest I kept looking at her, and my eyes grew to what one of the doctors said was the size of golf balls.

All of a sudden I passed out.

2 · Your Future's on the Line

The old cliché goes, athletics can save a kid. In my case, that was definitely true.

If it hadn't been for sports—football in the fall, basketball in the winter, baseball, softball, and basketball in the spring and summer—I'd have joined some neighborhood gang and *not* the YMCA when I was a kid. And today I'd probably be wearing a long number across my chest, the kind of number a lot of the kids I grew up with on Chicago's tough West Side—the Lawndale area, to be exact—are wearing these days. Or maybe I'd be dead.

Thanks to sports, I survived.

Not that I was Mr. Clean, Darryl Goody-Two-Shoes. I messed around plenty: I stole bikes; I beat up white kids in Cicero across the railroad tracks; I ripped off stores for stereos and records and televisions and clothes; I broke into railroad boxcars, stole what I could and then sold the merchandise for whatever I could get. A $500 television set would bring $50 cold hard cash, and that was a lot of money. Everyone in Lawndale did those things, and I was no different.

I was born in Chicago on September 18, 1951, the fourth and last of Harold and Hilda Stingley's children. I was *really* the baby brother of the family, too. My brother Harold Jr. was ten years older than me, my brother Wayne nine years older, and my sister Andrea was seven years older than me.

Next to football, my father's big sport was boxing, which, thank God, he confined to the gym. He never used his kids as punching bags and never practiced his left jab against the bedroom wall. Come to think of it, it was at a boxing event at one of the local park districts that he met my mother. She was fairly athletic herself, having been a gymnast and also a cheerleader during her high school days, and they hit it right off.

My father was always very active in athletics. Just before World War II he had been a good semipro football player for the Chicago Brown Bombers, an all-Black team, and supposedly had a chance to play in the NFL, or at least get a tryout. He weighed only 165 pounds and played safety on defense, end on kickoffs and left halfback on offense. Ironically he suffered a serious neck injury while playing in a game. A year or so later, against all his doctors' wishes, he was back playing football again—under the name of Jack, not Harold, Stingley, and the bio on him said he had graduated from Kentucky State. Actually, he never graduated from high school, having dropped out after his junior year to get a job. But it was easier for Jack Stingley of Kentucky State to play for the Brown Bombers than it was for Harold Stingley, high school dropout.

My father used to tell me that when he played football the only equipment he had, aside from his soft helmet, was cardboard pads under his shirt and chopped-up rubber mats as elbow and knee pads. He said to me, "Darryl, you're gonna laugh at this, but I rarely got hurt." My father was, and still is, definitely of the opinion that modern-day football players in their gladiator outfits had too much protection. "You take a football player today and bounce him on the ground. He'll bounce back twice as high, he's got so much rubber on," my father told me one day. He thought the younger generation was too soft, I guess.

All in all, I was born of two good and healthy parents with athletic backgrounds and athletic interests, which they passed on to their children. Harold Jr. was deep into track in high school, Wayne was a star running back for Marshall High in Chicago and a star defensive back for Eastern Illinois University. He also was drafted by the Dallas Cowboys as a defensive back but didn't make it in the NFL. I idolized Wayne, and he served as my role model in athletics. Andrea was a gymnast and a cheerleader in high school, just as Mother had been.

Our family wasn't rich by any means, but I don't remember ever being in desperate need of anything. My folks ran a happy household and always managed to keep food on the table and a roof over our heads. My father was without a doubt the hardest-working person I knew. He worked for a tea company that would get large shipments in from all over the world, then make these special blends and ship them around the United States. I still can hear him telling us how hard he worked, and how he thought we didn't quite appreciate his efforts.

One day he took me to the warehouse with him so I could see how tough his job really was. I was a young kid, just eleven or twelve, and pretty full of myself. He put me to work lugging these big fifty-pound sacks of tea from one place to another in the warehouse. God, I almost broke my back. I never worked so hard, never hurt so much, as I did that day. Then I looked at my father. He was well-built—6 feet 1 inch, about 220 pounds—with fantastic upper-body strength. There he was down in a pit, wearing a dirty old T-shirt and pair of pants, breathing the smell of tea, picking up 200-pound crates of tea and slinging them here and there as if they were feathers. I was impressed! Let me tell you, I was very humble that night on the way home.

I never wanted to get on my father's bad side because I knew that though he'd never do it, he could tear me into two million pieces in about two seconds flat. He talked to me a lot, giving me fatherly advice, and he was very clear about a few things: He never wanted to see me in a police squad car with handcuffs on. He told me I should always use my judgment when the thought of pulling some caper entered my mind, that I should act the way I had been taught and told to act. He told me that the world didn't owe me anything, that I should work for what I wanted, not take something from the person who rightfully owned it.

"If you get yourself locked up," he told me, "I'm not coming to get you. And when you get home, I'm going to beat the living hell out of you."

Staying on the straight and narrow was not easy around Lawndale, which was a very rough place to be living during the 1960's, particularly in the middle and late '60s, when the race riots were at their peak. There were gangs on every corner. You either joined one of the street gangs, or you got beaten up by a gang. The choice was yours. But I was lucky. I became known around Lawndale as the kid who could play football, basketball, and baseball better than anyone else. True or not (it tended to be true), the net result of my athletic prowess was that the gangs left me alone. One kid from a gang told me one night, "Stingley, we won't mess with you, 'cause you might be the one guy from around here to make good."

Another thing. I never thought of myself as either a leader or a follower. I always tried to walk down the wide stripe in the middle of the road, to straddle the fence. It was true that I didn't officially join a gang. It was true that I spent a lot of time working out at the YMCA on the corner of Arthington and Kedsey streets. But it was also true that I did my share of bad things.

Like stealing bikes. My father, remember, had told me that the world didn't owe me anything, so I didn't feel that I could ask him to buy me a bicycle. It was the mid-1960's, and the bike to have was the kind with high handle bars and a banana seat, which had just come out. All the kids I played ball with had one, and so did I.

None of us had bought them. We got the bikes by going across the railroad tracks to Cicero, to the white neighborhood, and stealing them. We'd spot a kid on his bike, knock him off, and ride it back across the tracks to Lawndale. No one ever got caught. The white kids were afraid to make a big issue out of it because they thought we'd come back and beat them up.

Luckily for me, my father never found out that I was ripping off bikes from the white kids. He also never found out when I had my first encounter of the worst kind with the local cops. I was an innocent victim, but I didn't think my father would believe me. I was coming home from the Y, and I stopped off at a little variety store on the corner of Grenshaw and Central Parkway, near where we lived. The store had a lot of pinball machines and other games, and it was the local hangout for kids. We used to joke that there were more soft drinks and more candy bars stolen from that store than any other in all of Chicago. Trouble was, there was so much gang activity in our neighborhood that sometimes there'd be members of different gangs in the store—and then there'd be fights.

I walked into the store that day, and a second later a squad car pulled up in front, four cops jumped out with their guns drawn, and all hell broke loose. The cops came into the store, looked around and began to search everyone. They found guns on a couple of kids, and some knives, but they didn't find anything on me. I was clean.

"I'm not with any of these guys," I kept telling the cops.

"Shut the hell up," they told me. I shut up.

They took me, along with everybody else, down to the stationhouse in the squad cars, then called my mother to tell her I was in the clink. Thank God my father was still at work. My mother and my sister came to the stationhouse, acting just the way you'd expect a mother and sister to act when they see one of their own in jail, surrounded by a gang of cops. You could hear my mother's voice three blocks away. My sister was making a lot of noise, too, but my mother sure drowned her out.

31

"My son's a good boy. He didn't do nuthin'. You made a mistake. You made a terrible mistake. Darryl's a good boy. He was just coming home from the Y. He wouldn't hurt a soul."

"Stop, lady, stop," one of the cops said to my mother, who was waving her arms and making a big scene.

"Ask these other boys," my mother screamed, "Darryl . . . he's a good boy. He wasn't with them. He's no hoodlum."

Finally, the cops let all of us go, but they warned us not to be hanging around the variety store—and not to be carrying guns around with us.

"I didn't have no gun," I said to one cop, a big red-headed Irishman.

"Shut up, you little squirt, or I'll—" I was out the door before he could finish.

My real bag was sports, not crime. First at the Gregory School on the west side of Chicago, then at Herzel in the Lawndale area, and later at the Julius Hayes Hess Upper Grade Center (that's junior high) over on Douglas. Forget readin' and writin' and 'rithmetic. I looked forward to recess and to lunch break so I could get out and play my games. Funny thing was, I had no real desire to play football when I showed up at Marshall High School for my sophomore year in the fall of 1966. Like most inner-city kids I wanted to be a basketball player; it is a simple—and inexpensive—sport. One ball, a couple of hoops—no sweat at all.

Football, on the other hand, was a pain in the ass. You had to have a lot of equipment and a couple of dozen players. Also, you couldn't play football in the neighborhood because the parks were either paved over with cement or covered with rocks and broken bottles. And who wanted to have a permanent bloody nose? Besides, basketball had kept me out of jail the week before school began.

The summer of '66 was a hot time in the city of Chicago, and the streets on the West Side were filled with people who were out of work. Ringing up false alarms was one way to pass the time; indeed, the sound of fire sirens blared steadily every night of the week.

One night in late August when a hook-and-ladder truck roared out of the neighborhood fire house, the back of the truck immediately went out of control, because there was no fireman riding and steering the rear end. The truck hit a street sign, crashed into a building, and then smashed into a woman. She was almost decapitated.

That was all the people needed to lose their cool on this hot-as-hell night. I was there with some friends, and everyone started to riot and go crazy. As I said, I wasn't real bad trouble by West Side standards, but I wasn't an angel, either. What I was into, most of all, was trying to take advantage of situations when they presented themselves. So when I saw some of the guys looting a store for stereos and televisions, I didn't walk by that store and say to myself, "Darryl, those dudes are goin' to get in trouble." I joined in on the looting. I made a big haul—radios, records, tapes, a television, a stereo—and started to run away, dropping two radios behind me. Unfortunately, what I ran into was a cop, and he had a gun in one hand and his club in the other. He took me down to the stationhouse in a squad car packed with a half dozen other looters, and when we got there the sergeant behind the desk asked us our names.

"Darryl Stingley," I said. The sergeant paused and scratched his head when he heard Darryl Stingley.

"Hey, didn't I see you play in a basketball game a couple of weeks ago?" What the cop remembered was that I had played against him in a charity basketball game between my junior-high team and a squad from the police department.

He took me aside that night and gave me a fatherly lecture, telling me what he'd do to me—and what the police would do to me—if I ever got arrested again. And he let me off, just like that. If it hadn't been for playing basketball, I'd have been locked up like a criminal. Simple as that.

The only reason I went out for the football team was because my brother Wayne promised he'd buy me a new pair of shoes if I just gave football a try. Wayne couldn't understand why I wasn't all gung ho to play football at Marshall and follow in his footsteps as the star of the team.

"I hate the game," I told him.

"Tell you what I'll do," he said. "You know those flashy new dress shoes you say you want? I'll buy 'em for you. All you've got to do is try out for the team for a few days."

That was all I needed to hear. Hey, when you're a kid, you've got to keep up with all the new styles; you want to be the clotheshorse of the neighborhood. I really wanted those flashy shoes to go with one of my outfits (which, by the way, I had stolen from a boxcar in Cicero filled with clothes headed for Montgomery Ward's). But I couldn't afford those shoes. The thought crossed my mind that maybe I ought to shoplift them, but there had to be an easier way. Ripping them off from a store sure seemed like a bigger crime than stealing from a boxcar.

So to get those new shoes, I tried out for the Marshall team. And because Wayne had played for Marshall, and because he had been such a star for Marshall, and because he had made such a great reputation at Marshall, the coaches didn't treat me like just another sophomore rookie. They thrust me directly into the backfield—not defensive back or something else unglamorous.

Because of my basic athletic ability, football came easily to me. I don't know why, and I don't want it to sound like I'm bragging, but I seemed to have an innate ability as a running back. I liked to run. I could run as fast as the wind. And I had an instinctive ability to elude people when I was running. So I stayed with it—and got those new shoes. (Come to think of it, if I hadn't needed those shoes, I might be playing pro hoops right now.)

I remember my first game for Marshall. I hadn't played any Pop Warner or other type of organized football, just the roughhouse touch-and-tackle stuff we played at Garfield Park and in the alleys between our apartment buildings. This was my real football debut.

The first time I touched the football, I scored a touchdown on a run of about 35 yards. I didn't run over anybody. I ran around them. I was only 5 feet 9 inches and about 155 pounds—and I wasn't stupid. I was scared to get hit and that made me a very elusive runner. I fancied myself as the next Gale Sayers, not the next Jimmy Brown.

As a sophomore I started every game; after the season I turned to basketball, my first love, and was sixth man on the varsity team. Wayne didn't like me playing basketball, and neither did the football coach, Jim Peoples. One day after basketball practice Jim came by the gym to talk to me.

"I don't doubt your ability as a basketball player, Darryl, because you do play the game very well," he said. "But you've got to think about the future. About college. About the pros. The National Football League. Darryl, you've got a great opportunity to go to the college of your choice as a football player, and that's an opportunity not many kids from this neighborhood ever get. The thing is, Darryl, you're, what, a five-foot nine-inch guard and there aren't many five-foot nine-inch guards playing major-college basketball or playing in the NBA. You can't call your shots in basketball. You can in football."

Jim's words seemed to make a lot of sense. I had been a star in football, but I was only the sixth man in basketball. Everyone knew that Darryl Stingley was on the football team; no one knew he played on the basketball team. Marshall High was a big place, 99.9 percent Black, with about 5,000 students, including 1,000 in my class alone, and notoriety was pretty much reserved for the big-name athletes. I really enjoyed the acclaim I got during my sophomore year, particularly having the cheerleaders and a lot of the other girls say to me, "Hey, Babe, how're you? How's it goin'?" That's where, when, and how Tina Newsome came into my life.

When I was a sophomore at Marshall, Tina—her real name is Martine—was a freshman. It was December 1966. During the football season Tina had gone out with John Murphy, our quarterback, while my number one lady had been Janice Baker. Several girls were tied for number two on my list. You know how it is when you're fourteen or fifteen. You never know whether you're serious or not. I had my first sexual experience when I was twelve, and there were always plenty of girls in the neighborhood who liked to fool around.

At the start of the basketball season I had shaved my head, as had all the other members of the varsity team. One day Tina came up to me out of the blue and said that she liked the way my scalp was structured. I liked the way she phrased that. Now that I think about it, it sure was strange that her first physical attraction to me was to my bald head.

One thing led to another, and soon the rumors started: Tina and Darryl, Darryl and Tina. I began to believe those rumors myself. So did John Murphy, who got very upset at me for stealing his lady. The word spread around school that I had stolen Tina from him, and all the other guys on the football team got mad at me, too. But as soon as John got himself another girl friend, which took all of about a week, everything was normal again.

Tina and I became inseparable. She lived in an apartment on the other side of Garfield Park with her parents and her five brothers. We hung around the playground mostly, or she came and watched me play hoops at school or at the Y. I wasn't working, so money was scarce. A big date, a really big date, was to go down to Tad's and get a two-dollar steak sandwich. The movies were too expensive.

I told Tina I was in love with her. She told me that she was in love with me. But what did we know about being in love? Nuthin'. We didn't know nuthin' about nuthin', as we used to say in

Chicago. You know how it is. You go to a dance, you rub up against someone, and suddenly it's: "Hey, Baby, she loves me."

When school opened for my junior year, I decided to put all my efforts into football and forget about basketball as a career. I had a great season as a running back, scoring more than a touchdown a game and leading the team in rushing. It was the best of times, and Tina was there on the sidelines in her cheerleader's outfit, rooting for me.

Toward the end of the season I heard from my first college recruiter. The team was practicing one afternoon after school, and I noticed this guy in a big blue-and-white parka standing by himself near our bench and writing things on a clipboard. My first thought was that maybe he was a spy from the school we were playing the next weekend. My second thought was that if he was a spy from our next opponent, he wouldn't be stupid enough to be spying on us almost from our bench.

The next time the starting offensive unit got a break, I tried to sneak up on the guy to find out what he was doing. But before I could say anything to him, he introduced himself to me. I never did catch his name, but he said he was a bird dog for the University of Colorado. I asked him what a bird dog was.

"A recruiter," he said. "Actually, I'm not a recruiter, just a graduate of the University of Colorado and a friend of the football program. I'm a football nut, and I check out a lot of the high schools around Chicago to see if there are any hot prospects for the university."

"Where's Colorado located?" I asked him.

"In Boulder, just outside Denver."

"It's got to be pretty out there," I said.

"You'd love it."

Hey, I didn't know Colorado from Maine, but suddenly my mind was filled with thoughts of wide-open places, tall trees, snow-capped mountains, deep canyons, fresh air. . . . You name it.

The recruiter told me he had sent my name and some news-

37

paper clippings with my game statistics to Eddie Crowder, who he said was the head coach at Colorado. Then he reached into his briefcase and gave me a little pin with a Buffalo on it, along with a personal letter from Crowder telling me that the Buffaloes—the Colorado team, I quickly guessed, was called the Buffaloes—were watching my progress.

We talked for a few minutes. Or, rather, the recruiter talked a blue streak about how great life at Colorado was for football stars and how Colorado could sure use a running back with my potential. I just listened. Then it was time to get back to practice, and the recruiter was gone. Afterwards I put that letter from Eddie Crowder in my back pocket and carried it with me until the ink faded. A couple of other schools wrote to me during the Christmas holidays and expressed their interest in, as they called it, "my future academic plans." Of course, what they really meant was that they were interested in my future athletic plans. It was really all heady stuff for a high school junior, and I was riding high for a couple of weeks.

Then, early in February of 1968, Tina told me she had a little surprise for me. She was pregnant. I was going to become a daddy sometime around my seventeenth birthday. I didn't know what to say. I was in a state of shock. The way I saw it, I wasn't ready to be a father. Not yet.

Tina's folks found out right away and handled it well. I tried to keep the news a secret, but my mother got a phone call from Tina's mother one day telling her that Tina was expecting my child. When I came home that night my mother didn't say much. She just kept asking me, "How could you do it? How could you do it? How could you. . . ."

My father didn't find out for several months. I certainly wasn't going to tell him. No way. I knew he'd be mad as hell when he found out and that all hell would break loose. But my mother must've told him, or maybe he heard it from someone in the neighborhood. People saw Tina and me together all the time, and they'd have had to be dumb not to know that she was carrying a child. Anyway, one night he came home from work and said to me, "Son, why didn't you tell me the good news?"

I gulped. I could tell he wasn't thrilled with the idea of becoming a grandfather to his seventeen-year-old son's child. Suddenly I was really scared of him. He had warned me that I shouldn't hang out in the streets, that I shouldn't mess around with girls, that I shouldn't be like my brother Wayne, who had gone off to college and gotten a girl pregnant.

"I didn't think you'd think it was good news," I said to him. He shook his head. And that was the end of it. He didn't get mad at me. He didn't punish me. He didn't do anything. He just said that he and my mother would stand by me and help Tina and me out in any way they could. It was fantastic. And man was I relieved.

Soon after Tina started to get big, violence erupted in Chicago again following the assassination of Martin Luther King, Jr. I was a young, impressionable kid at the time, torn between being non-violent and violent when everyone else seemed to be violent. I quickly reverted to an earlier leaning and began to take advantage of situations as they presented themselves. Essentially, I forgot everything my folks had taught me. I forgot about respecting other people's property. About respecting other people. I went totally berserk with bitterness because of what had happened to Martin Luther King, Jr. And I wasn't alone. Like almost everyone else I knew, I went out into the streets of Chicago and robbed and looted.

It was a black-against-white mentality. When white people would drive through Lawndale and come to a red light, we'd run up to their cars and smash in the windows with baseball bats. We'd open the car doors and snatch purses from the women and tell the men to hand over their money, or else we'd beat the hell out of them.

None of it really made any sense; we did it because it was the thing to do. We broke into clothing stores and stole stacks of shirts and suits. We used bricks and wire cutters to break into the boxcars on the tracks in Cicero—Silver City, as we called it—and came back with stereos and TVs and tapes. We stopped at nothing. To us, the whole city was fair game.

Then, suddenly, I came to my senses. One night I just said to myself, "Darryl, your future's on the line. You're about to become a father. You're a good football player with a chance to play big-time college ball and maybe even go on to play in the pros. Compared to everyone else around the neighborhood, you've got the world by the tail. Don't blow it now." And that was it for me. No more robbing. No more looting. No more nuthin'. I was going straight. At least I was going straighter than I had been going.

All this time Tina had been living with her family and I had been living with mine. We saw each other during school and I'd be at her house after school and for dinner and stay until it was time to go home, usually around eleven o'clock.

That summer Luther Bedford, our football coach at Marshall High, got me a job at the United States Tobacco Company. Coach Bedford really cared about the guys on the team. He didn't want us spending the summer hanging around the streets getting into trouble, which was an automatic, so he went to a lot of companies around town and got us jobs.

U.S. Tobacco paid me $100 a week to throw boxes of Copenhagen, Happy Days, and other kinds of tobacco down a chute to the packing department. The work wasn't that hard, but I couldn't screw around. I had to be there at 7:00 A.M. every day, and I couldn't leave until 4:00 P.M. I always felt like a rich kid on payday, but as soon as I got home I gave $50 of my $100 to Tina to help her along.

In September I went back to Marshall for my senior year, which, I knew, would be rough. I had football to think of and I knew the college recruiters would be watching and taping me in every game, so I couldn't afford to have any bad ones. I'd have to work hard in the classroom to get my grades to a level good enough to get me into college. And, of course, I would soon become a daddy.

Sure enough, that great event happened on October 9, 1968. I was at football practice in Garfield Park, when Tina's brother Randall came running on to the field and said to me, "Darryl, she had a boy!"

A boy! Geez, I didn't even know she had gone to the hospital.

Within seconds all the other guys on the team had heard the good news, and they all came over to shake my hand and pound me on the back and call me "Dad" and "Pa" and a lot of other things. As it was, I wasn't the only father on the football team; two other players also had children.

I left practice right away and went to see Tina and the baby at County Hospital. They were both fine, and that baby sure was a good-looking kid, the cutest little thing I had ever seen. And he was mine. He was ours.

When Tina became pregnant, some family counsellors had suggested to our families that we—Tina and I—ought to consider either abortion or adoption, but we wouldn't think of it. That baby would be ours. And now he was.

We had decided that if Tina had a boy, we'd call him Darryl Jr.—and so he was Darryl Jr. But I don't think I've ever called him that. To me, to Tina, to everyone, he's always been Hank. Why Hank? Well, Hank Aaron was my favorite baseball player, and I just liked the name Hank. That's all there was to it.

As I walked home from the hospital that night, I suddenly was hit by the huge responsibility facing me in the future. I was a father. I said to myself, "Darryl, now you know you've got to make it and make it big. You've got to use this new son to spur you on to greater things."

The thought of getting married never entered my mind. It was too early for that. I was only seventeen years old. Tina was just sixteen. As my father put it, "Two kids had a kid." Also, thank God, I wasn't getting any pressure to tie the knot from my parents or from Tina's. Both families knew that marriage probably would put an end to my dreams for a college football scholarship and pro career. So they didn't bring up that subject. Instead, both said they'd help us work things out. How's that for understanding.

I officially celebrated Darryl's birth a few days later when Marshall played Wells High in our annual homecoming game. I ran 83 yards for a touchdown early in the game and had four touchdowns in all as we scored a tremendous victory. I had dedicated the game to my son, and I brought the game ball to Tina's house that night and placed it in his crib.

He cried.

I had a frantic fall season, and so did Tina. She handled her new role as mother perfectly. To her, Hank was a baby doll, and she didn't want to let him out of her arms. But when I'd come over to her place after school or practice, she'd give me little Hank and I'd try to give him his bottle. More often than not he wouldn't take it from me, and I'd have to give him back to his mother.

"Darryl," Tina would say, "you just don't have it when it comes to feeding a baby." I guess I didn't.

Meanwhile, I was tearing things up on the football field, scoring a lot of touchdowns and running for big yardage in every game. For the year, I had an average gain of 13.1 yards whenever I carried the ball, which meant I gained at least a first down every time I touched the ball. All the Chicago papers had big write-ups on me. The word was that I was one of the two main targets for college recruiters in the whole Chicago area. The other was a flashy running back for Farragut High, which played in another city league. His name was Otis Armstrong.

In my senior year at least 150 colleges contacted me, and two dozen invited me to spend a weekend on their campus. Every school used the same pitch in its recruiting: Darryl, come to our school and you'll be a big star. The schools that really wanted me went so far as to call Tina's house and razz her with their recruiting pitches. One guy from the University of Wisconsin used to sit around Tina's place and tell both of us, "If Darryl comes to Wisconsin, we'll find a place for Tina and Hank to stay, too, and we'll go out to dinner all the time."

Notre Dame became interested in me, or maybe more interested in me, after I won the Rockne Award as the MVP for all the leagues around Chicago. The Notre Dame recruiters made a big pitch to my mother, even asking her what shoe size I was because they wanted to have a new pair of cleats ready for me when I showed up at South Bend.

It wouldn't be too cool for me to say now what I was offered to attend some of the schools that were after me, but cars were usually up front. At seventeen you are very impressionable, and the offer of new wheels can sure make a big impression. If you're good enough to start, particularly at running back, for a big-time school, you can always get yourself a new car. Some schools also promised favors for my family, particularly a better-paying job with easier hours for my father.

I tried to talk some schools into offering Tina a scholarship as part of my joining their football program, but I wasn't successful. One of the state schools, though, did offer one of my good friends, a lineman who blocked for me at Marshall, a full ride if he could persuade me to go with him. I wanted to help him, but I didn't like the school because it was a rinky-dink, dull place. When I went to visit the campus, there was nothing to do all weekend. Maybe I'd have gone there and been All-World, but I'd probably have been picked in the tenth round of the NFL draft.

College had always been in my head because my parents had put it there, and I knew what college had done for my brother Wayne. In the end, what it came down to was that I had a chance to go all the way and play in the big time of college football—and I took it.

Purdue University really wanted me. An assistant coach by the name of Ron Meyer had made me one of his two special recruiting projects. His other project was Otis Armstrong. Meyer told me that Purdue made great sense for me because Leroy Keyes and a whole bunch of other Purdue stars were graduating, and I'd be able to step right into the starting lineup as a sophomore. He told me that Purdue made even more sense for me because the campus, in West Lafayette, Indiana, was only a two-hour drive from Chicago, and I wouldn't be too far away from Tina and Hank.

I didn't need much more convincing. When I visited the campus, I liked it right away, everything about it. As a kid in Chicago I had always read about how the Big Ten was the biggest and the best college football conference in the country—and now I was being offered a full athletic scholarship by a school in the Big Ten. I also liked the Physical Education program I'd be studying; I saw myself as a teacher-and-coach down the line. (Purdue had a top phys ed program.)

I signed to attend Purdue. As it turned out, so did Otis Armstrong.

As for Ron Meyer, shortly after I arrived he left Purdue to join the Dallas Cowboys organization. He became the head coach at the University of Nevada–Las Vegas in 1973 and in 1976 was named head coach at Southern Methodist University. In 1982 Ron Meyer was appointed head coach of the New England Patriots.

3 · Welcome to the Real World

In late August 1969, I said good-bye to Tina and Hank and took off down I-65 to Purdue. The deal was that I'd live on campus—Otis Armstrong was going to be my roommate in the dorm—and Tina and Hank would continue to live with her folks. She'd try to visit on the weekends during football season, and I'd try to get home as often as I could during the off-season. It was the best arrangement we could make for all concerned.

Jack Mollenkopf was the Purdue coach my freshman year, and both Otis and I had a rude awakening when we showed up for the first day of fall practice. Mollenkopf and his recruiters had never told us, but they had recruited Otis and me to play the same position—running back. It wouldn't have been so bad if Purdue had used two running backs, but Mollenkopf always built his attack around one man, the fullback. In the Purdue scheme of things, the halfback was a blocking back and a decoy. I wished their recruiters had told me that before I signed on the dotted line, but as I discovered the hard way, they never tell you the truth when they want you. They just tell you what you want to

45

hear: that you're going to be a big man on campus as a football star. Once you sign, that's it. The game is over. The man who said he was going to take care of you on campus, the guy who spent all his time wining and dining you on recruiting trips, is nowhere in sight. He's off at some high school, shoving the same line of b.s. at some other high school hotshot.

That first day of practice Mollenkopf had the freshman coaches put me out at the receiver's slot on the weak side. Otis was the fullback, the main man.

"What the hell am I doing out here?" I asked myself.

In high school the quarterback had just tucked the ball into my belly and I had run away with it. We never passed the ball at Marshall High. Never. The only time I had ever been on the receiving end of the football was at the Y in Chicago, when Nick Seabrook, the program director, would open the doors at 8:00 A.M., two hours before the building was scheduled to open, and work out with me. He'd throw passes to me until his arm turned to celery. Now that I think of it, maybe Nick had an inkling that someday I'd be switched from running back to a receiver's spot and wanted me to be ready.

The Purdue coaches tried all kinds of positive-thinking psychology on me: "Darryl, you've got good hands"; "Darryl, you can catch the football"; "Darryl, we'll get the ball to you in the open and you'll only have one or two guys to beat"; "Babes, you were born to be a receiver, not a running back"; "Listen, Stingley, you'll get yourself killed if you play running back. The monsters from Ohio State and Michigan will grab you by one hand and fling you all over the field. Those guys take little guys like you and spit you out. Play wide receiver. It's safer out there."

I had a hard time coming to grips with all this. I wasn't bothered by the fact that the coaches had made Otis, who then was about 6 feet 1 inch, 205 pounds, and still growing, the number one running back. What bothered me was that O.J. Simpson was my new idol, and I wanted to be the I back, the big man in the backfield, and carry the ball all the time, just like O.J. did. I had visions of grandeur, of being the next O.J. Simpson.

I wasn't ready to be a receiver for Purdue, but I didn't have much choice. I was pretty light, only about 170 pounds, and in the Big Ten all the running backs were usually either bowling balls or these huge 230-pound studs. Me? I was a pedigreed racehorse. But for the time being, it was either wide receiver or the bench. As the saying goes, "It's the coaches' way or the highway." Actually, I thought of taking I-65 right out of West Lafayette and not stopping until I was back in Chicago. I told Mollenkopf and the coaches I was leaving Purdue and transferring to some other school that had been hot for me because he and his recruiters had shafted me. "You promised me I'd be a running back," I said, "and now I'm out there as a wide receiver—on the damn weak side of the field, and I don't even understand what the weak side of the field really means."

Then one of the Purdue assistant coaches laid it out, "Son, we never promised you anything."

That really got me going. Why, when they were recruiting me, they promised me the moon. Now they were playing a new game. But that night in the dorm I thought about what the assistant coach said, and it didn't take me long to realize he was right. Purdue hadn't promised me anything. Sure, the recruiters had *said* a lot of things to me, a lot of sweet nothings. But they had *promised* me nothing. They said that I'd play for Purdue and be a star in the Big Ten. They never said that I'd be the I back and carry the ball twenty-five times a game. I sure wished they'd told me how they planned to use me when they were recruiting me, because if I had known they were going to put me at wide receiver, I'd have gone somewhere else. But there I was, a freshman playing a new position. If I transferred to another school, I'd lose the equivalent of two football seasons, because I wouldn't be eligible for varsity competition until 1971. Also, it was too late to get into another school for the fall semester. And if I quit

47

Purdue, what would I do all fall? I knew the answer. I'd go back to Chicago, find a job, probably live with Tina and Hank someplace, hang out back on the street corners of the West Side and probably get caught up in the violence that was still running wild. I also figured that if I ever quit Purdue, I'd never go back to college. I decided to stick it out.

Freshman football was a big bore. In 1969 freshmen weren't eligible to play varsity ball, so like most Big Ten colleges, Purdue used its freshman team mainly to run the plays of the next opponent on the schedule. One week I'd be a wide receiver from Ohio State, the next week a wide receiver from Indiana, and the week after that a wide receiver from Notre Dame. It wasn't a whole lot of fun, and the guys on the varsity didn't make things any easier for the freshmen because they treated us all the same: like dirt.

Around the campus Otis and I became known as the Chicago Connection, because we were inseparable. Both of us really enjoyed the wide-open spaces around West Lafayette—at least wide open compared to the West Side of Chicago.

Tina came down a lot in the fall, and so did Otis's girl friend, Yvonne, whom everybody called Skip. We'd go over to the Greyhound Bus stop and meet them on Friday afternoons, and then show them a good time until Sunday afternoons, when they'd have to go back to Chicago. Once the season ended the routine was reversed: I was the one taking the Greyhound. As soon as class was over on Fridays, I'd hop a bus for Chicago and stay with Tina and Hank until it was time to return to school on Sunday night.

One weekend I showed up at my family's place and my father wasn't around, which was strange. He and my mother had decided to go their separate ways after almost thirty years of marriage. I was upset, but there wasn't anything I could do about it.

In 1970, rather than go home for the summer, I mostly stayed around Purdue and worked for the National Homes Corporation as a construction assistant on some of their home-building projects. I didn't know what kind of work I could get back in Chicago, but the Purdue football coaches always had enough jobs to go around for all the players. And because there were so many of us working around town, we were able to hold informal workouts four or five times a week, and I was able to develop my moves as a wide receiver.

I got home to see Tina and Hank every other weekend or so. Then, just when I was getting ready to go back to Purdue one Sunday night, Tina gave me the news: She was pregnant again. To put it mildly, I was not all that happy. Suddenly, I felt like my whole world was falling in. I started thinking that Tina was trying to keep me in a situation I didn't want to be locked into. I had found a whole new world at Purdue, one totally opposite in every way from the life I had known in Chicago. I was happy there. I had grown and matured a lot since leaving Chicago, certainly more than Tina had in that time. She had had one child when she was fifteen and now she was going to have her second at seventeen. I had gotten away from the ghetto and seen how the other world lives; she hadn't had that chance. Not yet.

So, I was going to be a father again, and with two kids and a lady to take care of, I couldn't be off leading the good life alone. I had responsibilities. The way I saw it, my game plan had been pushed into reverse and I didn't know what to do. Some members of Tina's family suggested I ought to drop out of Purdue and get a full-time job to provide for my expanding family. I thought about it; thought about it for a long time, but I came to the conclusion that I wasn't ready for all that responsibility. Not yet. I wanted to finish my education—and then let things fall into place. I don't think that I was being selfish, either. So, I went back to Purdue, and Tina and Hank stayed at her family's place. All in all, it seemed to be the best thing for everyone.

My personal problems—Tina's pregnancy and my parents' divorce—were forever on my mind, but I wouldn't let them interfere with my performance on the field that fall. I won the

49

starting job at wide receiver, and in our second game I caught nine passes for 85 yards as Purdue upset Jim Plunkett's Stanford team 26–14. Plunkett was supposed to be the best college quarterback in the country, and in fact he went on to win the Heisman Trophy as the best college player in 1970. When Plunkett was on the field, I studied him closely, to find out why he had gotten such rave reviews.

It didn't take long to understand why all the NFL scouts had unanimously rated Plunkett as the player who'd go first in the draft after that season. He threw the most perfect passes I had ever seen. He had a good dropback, and at 6 feet 2 inches and 210 pounds he was strong enough to stay in the pocket and fend off would-be tacklers until his receivers broke open. And when they did break open, Plunkett would get the ball to them right on their numbers. He threw soft passes, too, not bullets. God, I thought to myself, catching one of Plunkett's passes was like plucking a feather from the air. He always threw the ball to the correct side of the receiver, and on long passes he flat out flung the ball way down the field and had the receiver run under it.

Mind you, we had a pretty good quarterback ourselves in Gary Danielson, but Plunkett at that time was in a league of his own. I said to myself, "Darryl, someday, if you're lucky, you might get to catch passes thrown by a quarterback like Plunkett."

I was one of the top players on the Purdue team my sophomore season, catching 23 passes for 286 yards. I also returned eleven kickoffs for 181 yards and eight punts for 66 yards. Twenty-three receptions was considered a lot for anyone in the Big Ten, because most teams in the league, Purdue included, thought the forward pass was the worst thing that ever happened to football.

The Purdue coaches built much of our offense around Otis and me, and we were marked men every time we stepped onto the field. Everyone knew that Woody Hayes coached something akin to intimidation when he was at Ohio State. If you had a bad leg or something, Woody's boys always seemed to go right after it. Ohio

State was one of the best college teams in the country, and the Buckeyes' defense, which included All-Americans Jack Tatum, Mike Sensibaugh, and Tim Anderson, was one ferocious bunch. I think that most people—myself included—would tell you that under Woody Hayes Ohio State approached every game with the same sick attitude: "Let's get rid of the top players on the other team. Let's beat the living hell out of them. Let's send 'em home on stretchers." And what happened to Otis and me that day convinced me I was absolutely right.

It was easier for Ohio State to get Otis because he carried the ball every other play. They didn't put him out of the game for any extended period, but they did a heavy number on his body. I know. We were rooming together in an apartment just off campus, and Otis could barely move for several days afterward. He hurt all over.

Early in that game I had a hassle with Tim Anderson after he struck me for what seemed to be no good reason away from the play; a few years later Anderson was playing for the Minnesota Vikings and again he gave me a couple of what I thought were pretty cheap shots in a game. Ohio State players never grow up.

Then I met Jack Tatum for the first time. It was a third-down play, and my assignment was to block downfield. The man I was supposed to get was Tatum, the safety, and I threw a rolling block at his legs, just the way the coaches had taught me. It was an ordinary block, nothing unusual, certainly not vicious, but Tatum didn't like it.

"Whaddaya tryin' to do, Man?" he screamed at me. "You crazy or something? You know I'm getting ready to turn pro. What are you trying to get my legs for?" Fact was, I wasn't trying to get his legs or his arms or his head or anything else. I was just executing a simple block. I didn't say anything, just walked away.

We had to punt on the next play, and as I lined up along the line of scrimmage, who set up directly opposite me? Jack Tatum. He was jabbering away at me, trying to intimidate me. He told me in no uncertain terms that he was going to get me. And he did, a few plays later, with some help from his friends Anderson and Sensibaugh. They all got together and leveled me on a pass pattern over the middle. I couldn't even get to my feet until our trainers had given me a few whiffs of ammonia. Tatum had probably made his coach very happy. Why, Woody probably gave Tatum and Anderson and Sensibaugh one of those Buckeye leaf stickers for their helmets because they had knocked me out.

I was only nineteen at the time, and because I didn't know any better I returned to the game for the second half. Tatum was waiting for me. I ran a down-and-out, and just as I went to catch the ball at the sideline, he cracked me in the head and I went down in a heap. I almost swallowed my tongue. Cheap shot, yes. Personal-foul penalty, no. After a while I got up, and after staying on the sideline for a few plays, I went back into the game.

It was cold and snowing that day, and we played the heavily favored Buckeyes practically to a standstill, losing to a field goal in the last minute or so.

When the backslapping began after the game, Tatum came up to me and told me he had lost his head on the play on which he knocked me out. He didn't apologize for losing his head, just said that he had lost it.

"You lost your head?" I said to Tatum. "Shit, Man, I almost lost my head because you lost your head." I don't think he understood what I meant. I don't think he cared.

Jack Tatum was going to the Rose Bowl, maybe, and some postseason All-Star games, and then he'd be signing a big-bucks contract with some NFL team. Talk was cheap to Jack Tatum. Especially talk that meant nothing. Whatever he did or said, he must've gained a bit of respect for me. I never backed down to him or to anyone else in that game, and never would. If nothing else, I was one tough wide receiver.

On the whole, I had a pretty good time that fall. Each weekend of the football season when we had a home game, a carful of

Stingleys, Tina and Hank included, and a carful of Armstrongs, Skip included, came down and had a grand time with Otis and me. They'd tailgate and picnic before the game on Saturday, and then Otis and I would join them for a party after the game and do it up big all day Sunday. We were in a world of our own, and you couldn't beat it.

Academically, I was a fair student. In my mind my main missions at Purdue were to get my degree in phys ed and to educate myself as a football player, to prepare myself for a career in the National Football League. The demands of big-time college football were so heavy that, like all the other players on the varsity, I wasn't able to carry a full academic load. But I accumulated enough credits each semester to maintain my eligibility, and that, as the coaches always used to tell us, was the name of the game. Looking back at it now, I'd say that the name of the game should have been: Get your degree. But hey. What did we know? We all were along for the ride.

On April 7, 1971, six weeks before the end of my sophomore year, Derek Stingley came into the world. No one else in my family or in Tina's family was named Derek. We just liked the name Derek, so we named him Derek.

When I saw little Derek for the first time in the hospital, I quickly forgot about all my early bitterness and my resentments toward Tina, and was really proud, the same way I had been proud when I saw Hank for the first time. Once again I was under some pressure to quit Purdue and get a job and support my growing family but I refused. My brothers and sister had graduated from college and gone on to bigger and better things. They were my role models, and I'd follow in their footsteps. Tina would have to continue living with her family and raise the two boys. I would come home and take care of all of them when I could, which, the way I saw it, was the day some NFL team drafted me.

That summer I again worked in West Lafayette as a painter for the university, but got home to Chicago to see Tina and the boys just about every weekend. Then, when school resumed in September, Otis told me he didn't want to room with me anymore, that he had a new and better roommate. Over the summer he and Skip had tied the knot and they had rented an apartment just off campus. The fact that Otis and Skip were married got me to thinking that maybe I should marry Tina, but I knew I just wasn't ready for it.

On the field I had a dynamite junior season. We used the wishbone offense some of the time, and I got to play at running back as well as at wide receiver. I caught thirty-six passes for 734 yards—an average of 20.4 yards per catch, one of the best averages in the country—and had touchdown catches of 70, 76, 66, and 80 yards. I was easily the leading home-run receiver in the Big Ten and in fact made first team All-Big Ten, not bad for a mere junior. I also rushed the ball 60 times for 248 yards and three more touchdowns, giving me a total of eight for the season.

Once the season was over I began to get questionnaires from all the NFL teams, and the word was that after my senior year I'd probably be a first-round draft pick. To me, that meant one thing: dollars. Big dollars. Very big dollars. One of the questions on all those forms was: Did you or do you now have an idol? My answer was yes. The following question was: If yes, who and why?

My answer: Paul Warfield. I wrote, "I feel if you have an idol, he should be the best in whatever his profession is. Paul Warfield is the best wide receiver in pro football. I'd like to study him and learn from him. Perhaps someday I can be his equal." That was my ambition.

In the spring of 1972 the Purdue coaches brought in a guest instructor for the clinic that was part of our practice. At that time Chuck Fairbanks was the head coach at the University of Oklahoma, one of the best teams in the country. Chuck worked a lot with Otis and me, showing us how Greg Pruitt, who was playing for him at Oklahoma, ran certain plays and made certain moves. I guess we must have impressed Fairbanks, too, because when he was leaving Purdue to return home, he said publicly: "I'd sure like to take a couple of your players back to Oklahoma with me—Otis Armstrong and Darryl Stingley." I loved that. I figured that Fairbanks had a hot line to the pro scouts and that he'd be touting my name to them. Everything helped.

My final year at Purdue was pretty much of a bummer, athletically speaking. I missed the first five games of the season with a severly sprained ankle injury, and when I came back to the lineup the passing game was out and the wishbone running attack was in. I caught only ten passes but gained 236 yards—an average of 23.6 yards per catch—including one 79-yard grab for a touchdown. I ran the ball fifty-two times for 226 yards and another touchdown. That wasn't exactly the way I'd planned to wind up my college career, but the NFL scouts didn't seem to mind—and neither did the player agents, who hovered over Otis and me before, during, and after just about every Purdue practice and game. The scouts would show up with their little stopwatches and clipboards and mimeographed forms they wanted you to fill out. They'd time your break from the line of scrimmage; they'd time you for 10 yards, 20 yards, 30 yards, 40 yards. My 40 was a 4.35 on turf and a 4.40 on grass, and the scouts said that no wide receiver had a better time on grass than my 4.40. I don't know what they wrote on the papers clipped to their boards, but I'm sure it had to do with things like attitude and desire, in addition to ability.

The word I got from the scouts was that I'd go in the first round of the draft, somewhere in the second half, between the fifteenth and twenty-eighth picks. That made me happy. Very happy. First-round draft picks got the big bucks. The people who told me that were the agents and lawyers who kept bugging me to let them represent me in my contract negotiations with the NFL team that drafted me. Those agents came in all sizes and all shapes, but they all sang the same tune.

"Hey, I'll lend you some money if you need it."

"Hey, I'll buy you some clothes if you need them."

"Hey, need a car? I'll advance you the down payment."

"Hey, you want to take Tina on a vacation over Christmas?"

You name it, it was offered to me by the dozen or so agents and lawyers who sought my business. I finally wanted to see just what those agents really would give me, so early in November I said to one of them, "Gee, I'd like to make this Christmas a nice time for Tina and my boys. You know, buy them some nice presents and stuff." Well, the guy whipped out a roll of bills, peeled off five $100 notes and gave them to me without blinking an eye. Just like that. My eyes bulged out of their sockets. He tried right then to get me to sign some papers on the dotted line that would tie me to him, but I told him I couldn't sign anything. "You know," I told him, "it's against NCAA rules to sign with an agent before the end of our football season, and I've still got two games to play."

The guy said, "Don't worry about it, Babes. I'm not going to tell the NCAA nuthin'." And you know what? I took the money, but I never signed with that agent. And I never paid him back that $500, which I did spend on Christmas presents for Tina and the boys. The guy came to Purdue looking for me—and his money— after I made it known that I was going to have John Wooten represent me, but I was ready for him.

"Hey, Man, what do you mean?" I said to him. "I didn't get any five hundred dollars from you." Then I told him that if he harassed me for the $500, I was going to pull the rug on him with the NCAA and the NFL—with the whole world. Don't think I was the only college senior who pulled that sting on an agent, either. Everyone I talked to at the North-South Shrine Game in Florida and the Senior Bowl at Mobile—a couple of postseason college all-star games—told me they had done pretty much the same thing.

Only I hadn't hit up on my so-called agent for enough money. One player from a school on the West Coast told me he had ripped off a lawyer for almost $10,000.

After playing in the North-South Shrine game at Christmastime, I returned to Chicago and rented an apartment for Tina and the boys in the building that my mother and sister lived in. Tina had gone on welfare that fall to provide for herself and the kids, because the breadwinner of the family wasn't making any bread. But now I was in the bucks, having collected a nice check from the Shrine game and with another coming from the Senior Bowl and the biggest check of all coming after the NFL draft at the end of January.

Late in January, after playing in the Senior Bowl (I caught a touchdown pass in the game, which was watched by the largest live collection of NFL coaches and scouts and general managers and owners ever seen in one place), I went back to Purdue to wait for the NFL draft.

The night before the draft, I sat in my room and prayed that the Chicago Bears wouldn't select me. A lot of people like to come back from college and play for the NFL team in their hometown. Not me. The Bears had never been much of an offensive team, and their quarterbacks were terrible passers. Also, the Bears, because of Ol' Papa Bear himself, George Halas, were known as the tightest team in the NFL when it came to passing out money.

The morning of the draft Otis and I were in a class together when someone from the sports information office came to get him. It was Denver calling. The Broncos had made Otis their Number 1 pick. He was ecstatic.

When that class was over, I went home to my apartment and started worrying. It got to be 12:30 P.M., and some friends came by to cheer me up. At 1:00 P.M., the eighteenth player was selected in the first round and now it was Chicago's turn to pick number nineteen.

The phone rang in my apartment.

Oh no! Chicago!

"Hello," I said.

"Darryl Stingley, please," said the voice at the other end.

57

"This is Darryl Stingley."

"Darryl, this is the New England Patriots organization. Coach Fairbanks would like to have a few words with you."

Coach Fairbanks? It took a couple of seconds for that name to sink in, but then I remembered that the Patriots had just lured Fairbanks away from the University of Oklahoma to be their head coach and general manager. There was a long silence on the other end of the line, and then I heard Fairbanks's voice.

"Hi, Padnuh, how are you? Welcome aboard. It's nice to have you with us."

"Nice to be with you, Coach," I said.

We talked for a few moments. Chuck explained that he had traded one of his veteran running backs, Carl Garrett, to the Bears so he could draft me with that nineteenth pick in the first round. I told Chuck that I had enjoyed working with him at the Purdue spring clinic, and looked forward to playing for him in New England.

Then Chuck said that he knew I'd love catching passes from the Patriots' quarterback. Geez, I thought, who was the Patriots' quarterback? Then it came: Jim Plunkett. The same Jim Plunkett I had watched so closely my sophomore year when Purdue upset Stanford. The same Jim Plunkett who threw the best passes I had ever seen. "Right, Coach," I said. "That Jim Plunkett can sure throw a nice ball." Then Chuck hung up, and I sat down and began to think about what had just happened in my life.

Boston? Where was Boston? Better yet, where was this Foxborough, which is where the Patriots said they had their offices and played their games? I'd never been to Boston. Otis went there once to receive some award and wasn't wild about the place when he came back to Purdue. Now I was going to Boston, and he was going to Denver. I was envious of him. To me, Denver represented the great outdoors, the Rocky Mountains, Coors Beer, and a very laid-back place. Boston, on the other hand, was supposed to be stuffy. Then I thought about it some more. Hell, I had never been to Denver, and I had never been to Boston. You could have put me in downtown Boston and said I was in downtown Denver, and I wouldn't have known the difference. So why should I be bitching?

A couple of days after the draft the Patriots mailed me some clips from the Boston newspapers. The Patriots had had three first-round picks. The first man they drafted was John Hannah, the offensive guard from Alabama, the number one team in the nation. Hannah was one of Bear Bryant's good ol' boys. Second was Sam (Bam) Cunningham, the University of Southern California fullback who had been the Rose Bowl hero. It was obvious the press was really high on both of them. Fairbanks was going to rebuild the Patriots, and Hannah and Cunningham, said the papers, were going to be the cornerstones of his plans.

As for me, it was Darryl who? The fact that I was a wide receiver from a school in the Big Ten got a rise from all the columnists. I guess that back in New England everyone thought that all the teams in the Big Ten played like Ohio State and Michigan. You know, Woody and Bo—three yards and a cloud of dust.

I had picked John Wooten, the old lineman for the Cleveland Browns, to represent me in my contract dealings with the Patriots, and he quickly negotiated a three-year deal that called for a signing bonus of $45,000 and escalating salaries of $30,000, $32,000, and $35,000, plus some very modest bonus clauses. As soon as I signed the contract, I went down to a car dealer's and ordered a New Mark IV Lincoln Continental for myself. Then I went back to Chicago to see Tina, Hank, and Derek—and we all had a big party.

"Tina," I said, "this is only the beginning. Better days are ahead. For you. For Hank. For Derek. For me. For everyone."

4 · You Dumb Ass

My career as a New England Patriots wide receiver got off to an unavoidably late start. Along with fellow Patriot draftees John Hannah and Sam Cunningham and forty other NFL draft picks, I was selected to play for the College All-Star team in the annual preseason game in Chicago against the defending Super Bowl Champions, the Miami Dolphins. It was a thrill to be with the All-Stars and to play in a game that, over the years, had provided millions and millions of dollars for charities in the Chicago area. And it was a thrill to be able to perform as an All-Star right there in my hometown, before my family and friends.

But I'd have been a whole lot better off spending my time in the Patriots' training camp at the University of Massachusetts at Amherst and getting to know Chuck Fairbanks's offensive system. By the time we reported to camp, we were three weeks behind all the other players and felt we were out in right field someplace. I tried to catch up on the playbook by staying after the meetings and practices, but there was just too much to learn in too short a time.

We'd be in the huddle and Jim Plunkett would call a play; I'd

61

either line up on the wrong side of the formation or run the wrong route. The coaches weren't very happy with me, and the fact that I'd played in the Chicago All-Star game was no excuse to them. Fairbanks had brought in almost a whole new coaching staff, and there was pressure on them to get the Patriots winning. The team had finished with a 3–11 record in 1972, the worst in the AFC East, and Fairbanks didn't want to repeat that performance in his first year as the big boss.

A rookie's first training camp basically is a time to learn the team's system and make friends. The latter was easier for me than the former. A couple of days after I reported to camp the veterans sort of indoctrinated me into the club by getting me to sing my Purdue alma mater during dinner. Actually, I didn't really have an alma mater, since I was still thirty credits short of my degree from Purdue, but I did my best Ray Charles imitation for them anyway.

Besides learning the plays, I spent the preseason getting used to Plunkett's passes, which were even softer and more catchable than they had seemed when I saw him play for Stanford against Purdue. He was a receiver's dream. But every so often I'd have to catch passes thrown by our quarterback coach, Bill Nelsen, and, well, that was hell.

Nelsen had a strong arm but not much leg movement because of his bad knees, and he threw a textbook-perfect spiral every time. Trouble was, Nelsen's passes came at you like bullets. You'd hear them coming and you'd anticipate the pain—hisssss, smaaaaack, ooooouch! You'd catch the ball, but it would come at you so hard and so fast that maybe it could pull a bit of the skin off your hand. The pain would be awful. And the next time Nelsen would throw one of his hummers to you, maybe you'd give it the old short-arm treatment—and let it fly on past you.

Still, I managed to survive the exhibition season. Then we broke camp and moved across the state to Foxborough. I got an apartment by myself not far from the stadium. Tina and I had worked out a plan whereby I'd live in New England during the football season, and she'd live in Chicago with the boys. After the season I'd move back to Chicago and live with the three of them. We'd try it that way for a year, maybe two. After that? Maybe she'd move to New England. Maybe we'd get married. My future seemed pretty secure, professionally and financially, and I was getting to the point where I could think of getting married and know I'd be able to handle all the responsibilities that went with it.

Like every other rookie, I was really keyed up for my first regular-season game as a pro. We played the Buffalo Bills at home, and there were almost 60,000 people in the stands when we trotted onto the field a few minutes before kickoff. I was scheduled to start as the wide receiver, so I went right to the sidelines near our bench, grabbed a football and got Bill Nelsen to throw me a few quick passes, just so I could be all warmed up.

Nelsen threw me one pass after another in rapid-fire motion, and I picked them all off like cherries. He threw one spiral so hard, though, that when I caught it, it was still spinning in my hand. I squeezed the ball and it still spun. It pulled two of my fingers right out of their joints. I looked down and the fingers were just hanging there, limply.

Great! What a way to start your NFL career. Getting hurt *before* the opening kickoff! The trainers came over to inspect my fingers, and one of them ran over to Fairbanks to tell him that I was hurt and wouldn't be able to start. All year I played with my fingers taped together; nevertheless I had a decent enough season —twenty-three catches for 339 yards and two touchdowns—to make the NFL's all-rookie team and collect a $2,000 bonus from the Patriots.

Sam Rutigliano was the Patriots' receivers' coach my first few seasons. As a coach, Sam had his own personal game plan. Rather than become known as, say, a wide receivers' coach, Sam planned to switch his assignments every two or three years in order to gain experience in both offensive and defensive areas of coaching. That meant he'd probably have to move to a new team every two or three years, but it didn't bother Sam at all. (In fact, Sam was named head coach of the Cleveland Browns in 1980 after being a defensive coach for the New Orleans Saints for a couple of years.) Anyway, Sam felt, and rightly so, that I lacked development as a receiver, that I had great speed and could catch the ball with no sweat but I didn't know beans about the nuances of being a receiver. So he worked with me on my moves for hour after hour, showing me how to juke people out, how to fake and run, how to work the inside, how to read defenses, how to cut, everything. It was a whole new world for me.

Still, I became known in New England not for my faking and running but for my acrobatic catches, particularly after I made two one-handed, leaping-into-the-air grabs—stabs, really—for touchdowns in a game we lost to the Philadelphia Eagles. They were both unconscious reflex catches, not the type that can be taught. On both plays I went up, looked the ball into my hand, caught it with my hand totally outstretched, then cradled it against my body for protection. One of the Boston writers said that the only player who had ever made such catches in New England was Otis Taylor, and he played for Kansas City. Being mentioned in the same sentence with Otis Taylor made my day, my season in fact, because when I got to watch Otis work his magic against us as Kansas City beat us in the second game of the season, I immediately adopted him as my new idol.

We finished that rookie year with a 5–9 record, a long way from the Super Bowl but a hell of a lot better than the Patriots had done the previous year. Before I left Foxborough to go home to Chicago, Fairbanks called me into his office to give me his review of my season: He was pleased with my effort and my dedication, but I'd have to work even harder in 1974 to continue my development. He was upbeat, very positive as he talked to me, and I left for home with a warm feeling inside.

The play begins with Darryl split right, Tatum, the free safety (number 32), on the 13 yard line.

As the play develops and the ball is in the air Darryl cuts in on the 15 yard line, concentrating on the ball. Tatum, who has dropped back slightly, reads the play and begins to move in.

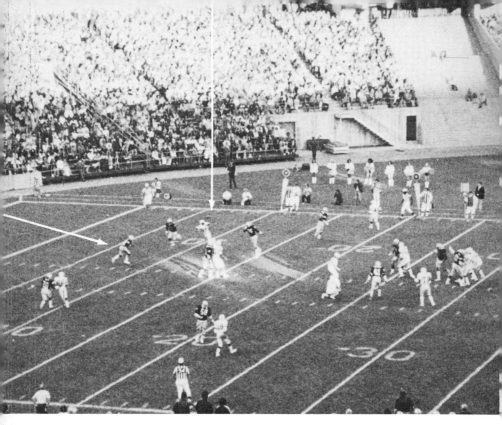

Darryl leaps for the ball. Tatum keeps coming.

With the ball already past and Darryl off balance from the attempted catch, Tatum goes for the hit.

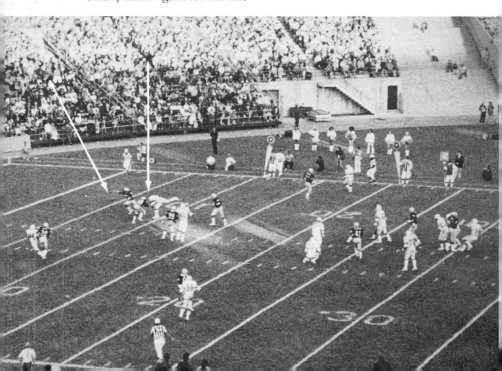

In closeup, Grogan drops back, Darryl leaves the line.

Grogan sets up, looking at Darryl, who's running the D pattern.

The ball is thrown.

Darryl gives it an all-out effort as Tatum comes in.

The ball goes by and Tatum sets up.

The Hit.

Tatum straightens up as the ball continues out of the play.

The aftermath.

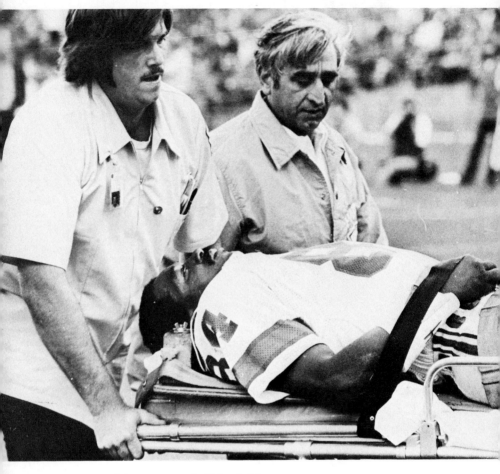

Darryl being carried off the field. *(UPI)*

During the season I came to admire Chuck not only as a coach—he had to be the most organized person in the world, and he never seemed to lose his composure when his rookies made their usual mistakes that hurt the team—but also as a person. Chuck made it clear that he didn't like to get too close to people, other than the members of his immediate family, but he let me get as close to him as I wanted.

I think the reason he looked out for me, took a special interest in me, was that his little son, Toby, and I had developed an instant relationship. Toby was my white shadow. He was crazy about me. He always wanted to follow me around, always wanted to carry my helmet or get me a drink during practice and after a game. During games, he'd always be alongside me near the bench, looking out for me, doing things for me. He was my buddy. I'd look around and I'd practically step on him, because he'd be in my back pocket. The coach saw this, and I think that's why he wanted to pull me into his fold. Mind you, Chuck never told me, or anyone else, how to lead my life; he just tried to show me how to act like a man, how to conduct my life in a proper, organized manner.

Chuck wasn't what you'd call real emotional, certainly not like a Vince Lombardi or a George Allen, but he got the best from you because he was always fair with you. If you weren't giving your best to him, on and off the field, he'd put his evil eye, as we all called that look of his, on you and you knew it was time to get your act together and produce. Or else you'd be gone. Nobody played games with Chuck Fairbanks and came out the winner.

Actually, Chuck described himself perfectly, if obliquely, one day that first season when someone asked him if he was going to attend some big sporting function in Boston, which was about twenty-five miles from Foxborough.

"I don't even know how to get to Boston," Chuck said. He wasn't being a smart-ass. What Chuck meant was that his life was all football and all family. He went from his home in Foxborough

73

to the stadium in Foxborough to his home in Foxborough—and that was his day, every day.

Fairbanks wrote me a couple of notes during the off-season, reminding me to keep in shape and work on the things that he and Rutigliano had told me needed work—my moves, disguising my takeoff from the line of scrimmage, my concentration on the ball. So I'd go over to the Y every day and have someone throw footballs at me for an hour, and I'd never take my eye off the ball. Never.

I couldn't wait to get to training camp, and when I finally showed up at Amherst in mid-July, I felt a whole new attitude in the air. Fairbanks had cleaned out the roster during the off-season, disposing of the players he didn't feel were committed to his game plan for success, the players he didn't feel were dedicated. Everyone in the 1974 camp was completely gung ho. And it showed during the exhibition season as we won four of our six games. We still didn't have many new believers out there, because all the experts picked us to finish last in the AFC East. But the easiest thing in football was to pick the Patriots to finish last since they had been close to the bottom, if not at the bottom, for more than ten years.

Surprise! Surprise! After five weeks of the season, guess what team was undefeated and riding high in first place in the AFC East? Guess what team had opened the season with a shocking 34–24 upset victory over the Super Bowl champion Miami Dolphins? Guess what team stunned the New York Giants 28–20 in their second game? Guess what team absolutely shocked the Los Angeles Rams 20–14 in their third game? Guess what team flat out trounced the Baltimore Colts 42–3 in their fourth game? And guess what team went down to New York and shut out Joe Willie Namath and the New York Jets 24–0 in their fifth game? That's right, the supposedly downtrodden, low-flying, miserable, woebegone New England Patriots.

We were the darlings of pro football, a first for any New England team, and we loved it. Fairbanks was being called a genius.

Jim Plunkett was being compared to the great quarterbacks in football history, the Sammy Baughs and the Johnny Unitases and the Bobby Laynes and the Joe Willie Namaths. One travel agency in Boston was even selling tours to the Super Bowl game in New Orleans.

I had caught ten passes for 139 yards and one touchdown in those first five games, but suddenly my season was over. I blamed it on the sophomore jinx. In that game at New York, the Jets set up a blitz and I had to adjust my pattern at the line of scrimmage in order to give Plunkett the opportunity to throw a quick dump-off pass, thus negating the blitz. Unfortunately there was some miscommunication between Steve Schubert, one of our other wide receivers, and me as to exactly where we both should go. As it turned out, we both ran quick slant-ins over the middle, Steve coming from one direction and me from the other, and we ended up in the same place at the same time. We really screwed up.

Two Jets were there with us, meaning there were four players practically standing next to one another. Plunkett, under a heavy rush, threw the ball, and the next thing I recall, I was sitting on the bench. I looked up at the scoreboard, saw it was the Patriots' ball, and said, "What am I doin' here? I'd better get in the game. Coach is going to be pissed that I'm not on the field."

I went to get up off the bench, braced myself, and then fell flat on my face. Kerplop. I looked down at my left arm and—ugh!— the bone was protruding through the skin. I almost passed out. What I didn't know was that I had broken my left arm and had also been knocked out during the collision with Schubert and those two Jets.

I saw films of the play the next day back in Foxborough. I was trained to go for the football. That was my number one job as a wide receiver: Catch the football. If I ran a pattern and looked at where everybody else was, then I wasn't looking for the football— and my chances of catching it, which I was paid to do, were slim. You can't catch a football unless you're concentrating on that football and only on that football. You also can't catch a football if you're worried about getting hit in the process. Because I had totally concentrated on the ball, I wasn't aware of the traffic jam over the middle. Then the four of us had this monstrous collision, and everybody walked away except me.

I had to wear a cast for three months, and became really depressed, not because I couldn't play football, but because I feared that my injury was worse than the doctors thought and that I might never be able to play again. I don't know how other players handle themselves psychologically when they're unable to play because of an injury, but I know what my reaction was: I brooded and worried, and then brooded and worried some more. The worst feeling in the world for an athlete is one of being helpless. I only had a broken arm, but God, did I ever feel helpless.

Even worse than that was the feeling I got while watching the Patriots play the rest of the schedule. After being the toast of the NFL with our great 5–0 start, we lost seven of our last nine games to finish the season with a 7–7 record. True, that was still an improvement over our 5–9 record in 1973, but not what we'd wanted or expected.

The football, as they say, takes funny bounces, and it certainly did while we were losing those seven games. We were blown away only once, by Oakland, 41–26. We lost to Buffalo twice, once by just one point, once by two points. We lost to Pittsburgh (which went on to win the Super Bowl a few weeks later) by just four points, 21–17. We lost to the Jets by five points, 21–16. And we lost to the Dolphins and the Cleveland Browns by the margin of a touchdown each. So close, and yet so far away.

My arm mended well during the off-season, and I worked out every day in Chicago to get myself ready for the 1975 season, which I thought would be the best yet not only for Darryl Stingley but also for all the New England Patriots. We may have finished the 1974 season on a downer, but we seemed to be on the verge of breaking into the upper echelon of the NFL, of being able to hold our own against the best teams week after week.

One reason for my personal optimism was that Tina and I were closer than ever and she had agreed to move to New England for the regular season; I'd be together with my family there for the first time. In the back of my mind I also was thinking about marriage, about making my arrangement with Tina legal. Things were all coming together, and I couldn't have been happier.

We rented a house, with an option to buy, on Torreyside Road in Brockton, a good-sized city about a twenty-minute drive from Foxborough. We enrolled Hank, then almost seven, in one of the city schools and Derek in a preschool program, and they appeared to love them. Life in Brockton was a big advancement for them, for all of us, in terms of education and style of living.

On the field, we won our two last exhibition games to finish the preseason with a 3–2 record. Everyone was optimistic about our chances in the regular season. One national publication was very high on us: "Look for the young upstart New England Patriots to make the playoffs in '75," it predicted.

I regained my job as the starting wide receiver, but didn't see the ball too much in our opening game, which we lost to Houston 7–0. A big upset. Then, in order, we lost to Miami, the Jets, and the Cincinnati Bengals, and after four weeks we were perfect: zero wins and four losses. The young Patriots sure weren't a bunch of upstarts! Worse still, our problems on the field were only minor compared to those off the field.

The Patriots had a drug problem.

One of our running backs brought plenty of marijuana and cocaine around, and it was available for whomever wanted or needed it; the guy had been busted when he played up in Canada, but the NFL had given him a clean bill of goods to play for us. One of our offensive linemen also got himself involved in some drug dealing and, as it turned out, had to spend the entire 1976 season in jail in Rhode Island. As a result, we all were under investigation, although the investigations—by state and local police authorities, the FBI, and the NFL—were never made public. Because of this we played under tremendous pressure all season. I was uneasy and uncomfortable, and so was Tina. And it didn't help matters when we found out that our phone was being tapped. It got so scary that I almost never used the phone, not even to call home to Chicago.

Midway through the season one of the Patriots' wives threw a Friday night surprise birthday party for her husband at their home in one of the towns near Brockton, and Tina and I were invited to go. But Tina didn't want to go. The Patriot wives, like the wives on all pro teams, were very cliquish, and Tina not only didn't fit into any of the cliques, she didn't want to be a part of them. So she went her own way and always stayed home rather than join the other wives at their various activities. We had a huge argument over the party. I tried everything I could to get her to go, but she wouldn't budge. I told her it was important that I be there—that *we* be there—because everyone else on the team was going and it would be good for team unity. She didn't buy a word of it. She kept telling me she was homesick, that she hated it in Brockton and couldn't wait for the season to end so we could all go back to Chicago. She even called my mother in Chicago and told her I was going to a drug party and wouldn't she talk me out of it.

I was furious and stormed out of the house alone. When I got to the party it was just after midnight, and there were more than a hundred people in the house. I didn't know half of them. Guys were running from one room to another. Girls, too. It was a wild scene.

I wasn't dumb. I had a pretty good idea of what was going on. The people in those rooms were probably doing cocaine. In those days cocaine was all over the place, not just in pro football. (Cocaine didn't just go away, either; by the early 1980s the stuff was so popular it was destroying the careers of NFL players left and right.) I stayed at the party for a couple of hours, drank a bunch of beers, talked to all the cheerleaders and a number of other ladies, and then left for home at about 3:30 A.M. When I got there, Tina was asleep. I thought to myself, "I should have been asleep a long time ago myself."

We had a game to play on Sunday, and of course we lost big. I hate to say it, even now, but the 1975 New England Patriots flat out quit. Gave up. We were a bunch of losers. The day after that game I came to the stadium for practice and was sitting in a special team meeting when Jim Valek, Chuck Fairbanks's right-hand man, stormed into the room and called out a bunch of names, mine included. "Coach wants to see you guys upstairs in his office, one by one," Valek said. I was the lucky one who got to see Fairbanks first.

As soon as I walked into his office, Fairbanks gave me his evil eye and began to scream at me. "You dumb ass," he said. "Don't you have better sense than to show up at parties where there are a lot of people you don't know and where a lot of funny things are going on?"

"Coach," I said, "I didn't want to be the only one on the team not to go."

"You dumb ass," Fairbanks said again. "There were a lot of guys on the team who were smart enough not to go." It suddenly became clear that at least one person at that party had reported everything that went on to the coach. Fairbanks then looked down at a piece of paper on his desk and lit into me again. "You got there about twelve-thirty A.M. and left about three-thirty. You had a helluva time, too. The only good thing is that you never went into any of those rooms where people were doing drugs."

"That's right, Coach," I said, "I never did any of that stuff."

"No, you didn't," Fairbanks said, "but you're a dumb ass anyway." Chuck lectured me for ten minutes about the evils of drugs, about the evils of associating with the wrong people. He told me that people would stop at nothing if they could ever use a football player for their own purposes. He told me I had to be on guard all the time, that I would always be a target for people who were up to no good. When I left his office, I was shaking. Chuck had told me he was going to get rid of any player he knew, or even suspected, was involved with the drug scene. I had been to that party, and I thought I was going to be on my way out of New England. The only good thing was that the NFL's trading deadline had passed, so the Patriots would have to keep me for the rest of the season unless they just wanted to release me and everyone else who went to the party.

The more I thought about that, though, the less I thought about it. If Chuck released all the men who'd been at the party, he wouldn't have enough players to put on the field for our game that Sunday against the Dallas Cowboys.

That Dallas game turned out to be the highlight of our season, if there was such a thing. We were big underdogs, as usual, but played the Cowboys tough for sixty minutes and lost by just a field goal. I scored two touchdowns and had a great day both catching the ball and running my end around on the reverse plays that Plunkett liked to call.

Unfortunately for Jim, though, that Dallas game pretty much marked the end of his career with the Patriots. As the team foundered, the crowds at Foxborough got more and more unruly and more and more hostile with their remarks, most of which were directed at Plunkett, who was highly sensitive. The crowds booed him mercilessly and started to yell, "We want Grogan, We want Grogan"—meaning Steve Grogan, the rookie from Kansas State who was Plunkett's backup.

Well, they got Grogan for most of the last five games of the season following our near miss against the Cowboys, but Grogan couldn't do things any better than Plunkett. Listen, you could have taken the best quarterbacks ever to play the game and put them in a New England uniform and we still wouldn't have been winners that year. That's how screwed up we were.

I finished the season with twenty-one catches for 378 yards and two touchdowns, but the team wound up with only three victories and eleven losses—and finished last in the AFC East. After two years of progress, we had returned to those lousy days of yesteryear when, as the newspaper writers said, the Pats were patsies. I was never so glad to see a season end as I was the day Baltimore routed us to write *finis* to the 1975 schedule.

After that last game I put Tina and the boys into the car and drove back to Chicago for the holidays. All the way there, as we drove through one snowstorm after another, Tina kept telling me how much she hated it in New England and how much she wanted to stay in Chicago. I told her that she hadn't given New England a real chance but if she still felt that way after school ended in June, she could move back to Chicago with the kids and I'd get just a small apartment for myself in New England during the season.

When we arrived back in Brockton after New Year's, there was a sick surprise in store for us. Someone had broken in through the windows in our basement and stolen all the kids' toys, my stereo and TV, all our books, and many of Tina's personal possessions, including her jewelry. Also, the pipes had burst, and there was eight feet of water in the basement. We had been wiped out.

"I can't take it anymore," Tina screamed. I had to sympathize with her.

"Man, the hell with this," I said, "we're going back to Chicago." You could almost hear Tina and the boys cheering in the background. I packed all our things into the back of a twenty-foot U-Haul truck, hitched it to the car, and took off for Chicago the next day. We were going home. Besides, in the back of my mind I had an idea that Fairbanks was going to trade me when he purged the Patriots of the players who had been at the drug party in midseason, so what was the sense of living in New England if I wasn't going to be playing for the Patriots?

Yet six months later there I was, back in training camp with the Patriots. As expected, a lot of old friends were missing, including some who hadn't gone to the party in '75. Even Jim Plunkett was gone, and I never expected that. In a blockbuster deal, Fairbanks had traded Plunkett to the San Francisco 49ers for a whole bunch of number one and number two draft choices. Steve Grogan now was our number one quarterback.

Grogan was no Plunkett when it came to the fine art of throwing a football. No quarterback was. But whatever throwing deficiencies Grogan had could be overlooked by the coaches because he was an intelligent, take-charge leader who had a natural, uncanny running ability that added an exciting, unpredictable, and at times unstoppable element to the offense. The coaches thought it would be hard to prepare a game plan to defend against the Patriots because no one knew what Grogan might do on any particular play. Why, Grogan himself didn't even know!

I was a perfectionist about my football, about learning my position, and I couldn't understand why the coaches hadn't been able to work out Steve's flaws as a passer. His major problem was that he threw a floater, a ball that travels with the nose up. Floaters are out of control and have no real authority to them as they travel from the quarterback to the receiver. Mind you, a floater is fine on a deep pattern, because the ball can take off and float down the field, allowing the receiver to run under it. But on the shorter timed patterns, passes under 30 yards, a floater is the last thing the receiver wants to see.

From a technical standpoint, it seemed to me that Steve threw floaters all the time because he had his hands in the wrong place—down around his shoulders, not up behind his ear—when he cocked the ball to release it. As a result, the ball tailed up and away from the receiver and was very difficult to catch. I remember a game at Buffalo when Steve threw a screen pass to Cunningham in the backfield and the ball kept floating and floating—nose up all the while—away from Sam for what seemed like forever. By the time Sam caught it, Mario Clark of the Bills was there to level him. Sam got smashed in the kneecap and his head hit the ground what seemed like two or three seconds before his feet. It was a wipeout.

When we watched the game films the next day, everybody oohed and aahed when they saw Clark's hit on Cunningham. Everybody, that is, except Sam.

"Hey, Steve," one of the coaches said to Grogan while the film was running, "you've got to keep the ball down on your passes and protect your players." That was all they said to him.

A couple of days later at practice, Grogan threw his usual floater to Sam on a screen play. If it had been a game situation, Sam would have been racked up again. He had to wait and wait for the ball and finally tracked it down by making a semiacrobatic catch. Sam was really pissed off.

"Hey, Grogan," Sam shouted. Everything on the practice field suddenly stood still; it was like the Twilight Zone. "You gotta keep that ball down, Grogan, or you're gonna get someone hurt—just like that pass you threw to me the other day in Buffalo." It wasn't a mean exchange, but the tone of Sam's voice was convincing.

Fairbanks and some of the other coaches rushed over. Then it was, "Okay, guys, let's go, back to work. . . ."

I was glad Sam had taken some initiative. The coaches never did. Never. Not that Sam's words did much good. Grogan kept throwing his floaters because he didn't know how to throw the ball any other way. And no one taught him anything different.

As for me, I kept trying to catch his passes. Nobody ever told the press that I had a remarkable ability to adjust to the ball, to react to where the ball was and somehow catch it. I know a lot of receivers who would have short-armed some of the floaters I caught from Grogan (or tried to catch but couldn't because the ball was too far over my head) because if they had gone up for the ball, they would have left themselves vulnerable to a heavy hit.

When Randy Vataha, Plunkett's favorite receiver, played for the Patriots he caught most of Plunkett's passes over the middle by sliding—not leaping. Plunkett always had the good sense to throw the ball low rather than leave his receiver dangling in midair trying to catch the ball. And Plunkett didn't throw floaters.

Adding to the receiver's risk of injury was the fact that the Patriots worked their pass patterns to the middle of the field maybe 80 percent of the time. That offensive strategy made it even harder for me to understand why the coaches never worked with Grogan to rid him of the floater. If you have to wait for the ball over the middle, or track it down, or go high for it—and one of these circumstances was usually the case when Grogan was throwing—then you're in no-man's-land and a candidate for a serious injury.

The Oakland Raiders, on the other hand, rarely worked the middle, preferring the down-and-out and the down-and-deep patterns. The Raiders wanted to keep their great receivers— Freddy Biletnikoff, Cliff Branch, Dave Casper—healthy, and one way to do that was to keep them out of the middle and away from the strength, numerical as well as physical, of the defense. Oakland's philosophy was to attack the sides of the field. New England's was to throw the ball into the middle, hope somebody would make a good catch, and then get a good block and break away for a big gain. Which philosophy was better? Oakland ranks with Dallas as the NFL's two most successful teams since 1965. The Patriots rank way down at the bottom.

During training camp I got a visit one day from Charles Jackson, who headed the NFL's drug investigation unit. He did all the talking, and I did all the listening. He told me to remember how lucky I was still to be around. He told me to avoid parties where there were drugs. He told me that one wrong move and Fairbanks would have me out of the NFL, out of football, quicker than I could blink my eyes. I believed him.

A few days before the '76 season opened, I was shopping at a mall near the stadium in Foxborough when I came across a poem printed on a big card. I read it, read it again, read it a third time. There was more meaning in that poem than I could imagine. I bought it, took it to the stadium the next day, and taped it to the shelf of my locker in such a way that I could read it every day. And I did. Here it is:

> *When things go wrong, as they sometimes will,*
> *When the road you're trudging seems all up hill,*
> *When the funds are low and the debts are high,*
> *And you want to smile, but you have to sigh,*
> *When care is pressing you down a bit,*
> *Rest, if you must—but don't quit.*
>
> *Life is queer with its twists and turns,*
> *As every one of us sometimes learns,*
> *And many a failure turns about,*
> *When he might have won had he stuck it out;*
> *Don't give up, though the pace seems slow—*
> *You might succeed with another blow.*
>
> *Often the goal is nearer than*
> *It seems to a faint and faltering man,*
> *Often the struggler had given up*
> *When he might have captured the victor's cup.*
> *And he learned too late, when the night slipped down,*
> *How close he was to the golden crown.*
>
> *Success is failure turned inside out—*
> *The silver tint of the clouds of doubt—*
> *And you never can tell how close you are,*
> *It may be near when it seems afar;*
> *So stick to the fight when you're hardest hit—*
> *It's when things seem worst that you mustn't quit.*

To me, that poem said it all.

We were a clean team off the field in 1976. We also were a together, unified team. In his early years with the Patriots, Fairbanks had held a team party at his home, something that gave the coaches and their families a chance to meet socially with the players and their families. I always thought it was a positive thing, a good show of togetherness. But for some reason Chuck didn't have his party in 1975. Maybe he knew of the drug problem before it became the major topic of conversation around the team. One day early in the 1976 season I said to Toby, "Why don't you ask your father to have another team party?" Two weeks later he had it, and everyone was there. It sort of set the tone for the season. We were a happy bunch, all committed to one thing: football.

The result was that we were a wild, exciting team on the field. And we were successful, too. We turned everything around, taking that horrible three-win eleven-loss record of 1975 and making it eleven wins and three losses in 1976. We made the playoffs—a first for the Patriots' franchise since the 1968 merger between the NFL and the AFL. There was football madness all over New England! It carried over to the players, too, and we were on a high as we flew out to Oakland to play the Raiders in the first round of the playoffs. To a man, we were all thinking Super Bowl.

In a midseason game at Foxborough we had whipped the Raiders by more than forty points. It was Oakland's only loss of the regular season and the most humiliating defeat in the team's history. And in that playoff game it was more of the same for most of the afternoon until . . . well, let me put it this way: The New England Patriots got screwed by the officials in every way.

We roared out to a big lead over the Raiders. Then, in the fourth quarter, they came with a rush as Kenny Stabler got his aerial circus together. But we still had the lead and the football until, on a crucial third-down play, one of their linebackers, Phil Villapiano, flagrantly held Russ Francis—held really wasn't the word for what Villapiano did; he manhandled Russ, he was all over him—right there in full view of the zebras. In one of the greatest heists I've ever seen, Villapiano got away with it. Grogan threw the ball to Francis, but there was no way Russ could escape from Villapiano's tentacles to catch it.

The replay of the Villapiano-Francis encounter was shown over and over again on the live telecast and later that night and all the next day on the highlight shows, and every commentator was quick to state that the Patriots had been royally screwed by the refs.

Earlier in that same game Francis apparently had suffered a busted nose when he was hit illegally—again in full view of a zebra who wouldn't drop his flag—over the middle by Oakland's George Atkinson, the defensive back who taught Jack Tatum all the "legal" tricks he didn't learn back at Ohio State. I never understood why the NFL let the Raiders, particularly Atkinson and Tatum, get away with all their cheap shots. It was as though there were two sets of rules, one for Oakland and one for the other twenty-seven NFL teams. When you played the Raiders, it seemed to me and most people that the referees usually worked by the law of the jungle.

That noncall against Villapiano stopped us in our tracks, and we missed a field goal from midfield. Then Stabler took over and drove the Raiders almost the length of the field for the winning touchdown in the final seconds. Stabler also had help from the referees, who made not one but two highly controversial calls against us. On a fourth-down play, Stabler threw an incomplete pass, but one of the zebras called our Sugar Bear Hamilton for roughing the passer—and then tagged on a 15-yard unsportsman-like-conduct penalty when Sugar Bear rightfully bitched about the roughing call.

That setback was a bitter pill for all of us. We had thought that maybe we were destiny's darlings at last and that all we needed to win the Super Bowl was a break. The ones we got, though, were not the kind we wanted. As it turned out, Oakland went on to win the Super Bowl by beating Minnesota. It was a hard game to watch since I kept thinking we should've been the team on the field—not the Raiders.

As for me, I led the New England wide receivers in '76 with

seventeen catches for 370 yards and scored four touchdowns. But in the end all the glory turned to sorrow, and the personal statistics didn't mean much. It was a long trip home to Chicago after our breakup parties in Boston.

Aside from that playoff loss to Oakland, the only real downer of the 1976 season was the fact that I was a lonely man. Tina had stayed in Chicago with the boys, and I was by myself in an apartment. Oh, I got out and around enough, but I would have preferred having Tina, Hank, and Derek with me all the time. Once I got back to Chicago I spent the next few months trying to persuade Tina to come and stay with me during the 1977 season. She'd have none of that. She said that Chicago was her home and that all New England did for her was make her homesick. It looked as if '77 was going to be just as lonely as the year before.

When training camp opened in the summer of 1977, we were still feeling good as a team. We knew we had the personnel and the potential to win the Super Bowl, particularly because we knew we had better players than the Raiders, and they had won the Super Bowl just six months earlier. All we needed was a good break. Any kind of good break. The trouble was, almost immediately things began to go against us.

The left side of our offensive line was anchored by two All-Pros, tackle Leon Gray and guard John Hannah. They were the best players at their respective positions in the entire NFL. Ask Sam Cunningham. Running behind Leon and John was a dream. They didn't open holes; they opened canyons. As for pass blocking, you know how the TV announcers like to say, "He had all day to get that pass away?" Well, with Gray and Hannah blocking for him, Grogan had all year to get off most of his passes. And, of course, that made things all the better for receivers like me.

Trouble was, the Patriots decided to play hardball with both Leon's and John's contracts, and whatever good team feelings we had suddenly eroded when both men walked out of training camp and then sat out several of our early-season games. Without them, our offense went *pffft*. We barely scraped past Kansas City 21–17 in our opener and then were upset two weeks in a row by the same 30–27 score, first by Cleveland, then by the New York Jets. Once Leon and John were back in the lineup, we won four straight games and eight of our last eleven, but that gave us only a 9–5 record—and we didn't even make the playoffs.

One thing I've never understood about the Patriots, and still don't, is why they let their contract problems spill over into the actual season. The Gray and Hannah situation should have been settled long before we ever opened training camp. Hey, we weren't talking about a couple of backup players. No other NFL team would have permitted a contract squabble to ruin its season, yet there was no doubt whatsoever in anyone's mind that the Gray and Hannah mess destroyed our 1977 season.

Once a season begins, a player ought to be able to concentrate on football and put everything else, particularly financial problems, out of his mind. Unfortunately, the Patriots have never operated that way, preferring to let contract problems intrude on the playing season—with predictably disastrous results. In fact, a few years after the Hannah and Gray disaster, the Patriots tried to play the same type of financial hardball with Sam Cunningham, so Sam sat out an entire season. And the Patriots needed Sam in the lineup. (Now, that may be changing, at long last. In the spring of 1983 the Patriots quickly wrapped up contract negotiations with Stanley Morgan, their great wide receiver, and several other key players. Then, to top it all off, they broke the bank to sign their number one draft pick, quarterback Tony Eason of Illinois, to a four-year contract for a reported $2.3 million. There seems to be a whole new attitude at work in Foxborough.)

I had my best season in 1977, catching thirty-nine passes and remaining injury-free for all sixteen games. For the first time, I seemed to put everything together. Whatever. In spite of all the good work, I failed to make any of the All-Pro teams or get invited to the Pro Bowl, both of which came as blows to my ego. Ron

Erhardt, our offensive coordinator, came to me a few days after the season and told me I had been flat out screwed by the people who had voted for the All-Pro and the Pro Bowl teams, that I had put together an All-Pro and a Pro Bowl season and deserved the recognition. "Darryl," he told me, "as far as we're concerned, you're an All-Pro."

I went home to Chicago again for the off-season, but it was going to be my final winter in the Windy City. At long last Tina and I were ready to tie the knot and become legitimate. I also had convinced her to return and live year-round in New England, and the Patriots were willing to renegotiate my contract and give me a long-term deal, one that would keep me in New England for at least five years. I also had a job interview set up for September with Dow Chemical in Boston and was told that the interview could lead to an off-season job and later full-time employment after my playing days were over.

So things were looking up when I drove back East for training camp in 1978. I spent several days checking out the Foxborough real estate market, and after looking at about a hundred condominiums I put a down payment on a condo in Stoughton, Massachusetts, about fifteen miles from the stadium. It would be home for all the Stingleys, who would be joining me sometime around Labor Day, when training camp broke up, just in time to begin the new school year.

My contract negotiations with the Patriots were intriguing, to say the least. My salary in 1978 was going to be only $52,000, a bargain-basement price for a receiver who the team's coaches thought should have been All-Pro. But I had a new attorney-agent representing me now, Jack Sands of Boston, and we approached the negotiations in a very low-key manner. We weren't shooting for the moon. We just wanted a fair and just salary, one that befitted my past performance.

Fairbanks was the general manager as well as the head coach, but he did not directly involve himself in salary discussions, leaving that job to Jim Valek, the assistant general manager. It made sense. A coach has to keep boosting his players and telling them how good they are; a general manager has to run a fine line, boosting his players on the one hand and knocking them on the other in order to keep the team's salary scale down. By having Valek do the negotiating, Chuck could tell the players to blame Valek if they didn't like their contracts. So Valek did the dirty work face to face, then went to Chuck and Billy Sullivan, the owner of the Patriots, for approval or, as often was the case in New England, disapproval. I don't know for sure, but I suspect it was always Sullivan, not Fairbanks, who made the final decision. It was his money, after all.

Valek opened our negotiations by offering me a three-year extension, starting in 1979, at annual salaries of $75,000, $85,000, and $95,000. We told Valek that his numbers were too low. Valek countered by telling us that while I had caught thirty-nine passes in 1977, I also had twelve dropped balls.

Great, I had twelve dropped balls. He didn't say how many of those twelve drops were passes that weren't spirals, or passes where I was going up for a rebound or a deflection, or passes that were at my outstretched fingertips, or passes that had arrived a few seconds too late. He also didn't say how many of my thirty-nine catches had come when I had to leap into the air or dive into the grass or turf for a poorly thrown ball.

Our discussions lasted throughout the first two weeks of training camp but fortunately didn't affect my performance or my attitude on the field. Every day or so Fairbanks would tell me how impressed he was with my dedication, my attitude, and my conditioning. Chuck must have said the same thing to Valek and to Billy Sullivan, because the day before the Patriots were scheduled to fly to California to play their first two exhibition games, Valek called Sands and asked him to come to training camp so they could finalize my contract.

Sands drove down to camp the next morning. We listened to

the Patriots' proposal and they listened to our suggested altera-
tions to the numbers. It didn't take long for us to reach an
agreement. The big number was $500,000 in salary over five
years, with bonus clauses that could earn me as much as $19,000
more each season. There was a $5,000 bonus if I was among the
top receivers in the AFC; $3,000 if I led the Patriots in receptions;
$5,000 if the Patriots won eleven games and I participated in 50
percent of the offensive plays from scrimmage; $3,000 if I was
chosen All-AFC first or second team; and $3,000 if I was chosen to
go to the Pro Bowl. Valek said he would draw up the necessary
papers and get them to Sands for my signature by the time the
team returned from California.

I was one very happy player as I walked out of the dorm at
Bryant College to get on the bus that would take us to the airport
for the flight to California. The new contract would be "guaran-
teed" too, meaning that I would be paid in full even if I suffered a
career-ending injury during the life of the contract, or if the club
for some reason decided to release me.

Jack Sands walked with me to the bus. "Take care of yourself,"
he said to me. "Be careful. Everything's going your way now. Tina
and the boys are moving here. You've got the contract you want.
Your future has never looked better."

"I know, Jack, don't you worry about me. Everything'll be
okay."

Jack smiled. "When you come back, we'll wrap up the contract.
Take care of yourself on the coast. And whatever you do, don't
break your ankle."

"Don't worry, I won't."

I got on the bus, waved good-bye to Jack—and it was "California, here I come."

5 · What's Happening to Me?

"Good morning, Mr. Stingley," the voice said.

Good morning? What did she mean, good morning? It was Saturday night, and we were playing the Oakland Raiders, about to go in for a touchdown. Good morning? It was night, not morning.

Wait a minute. Where am I? Why am I flat on my back, in bed, staring at a white acoustical ceiling? Why is this lady in a white coat saying, "Good morning, Mr. Stingley."

It had to be a dream. A bad dream.

I tried to move my head, to check out my surroundings. My head wouldn't move. Not an inch. I tried to lift up my right arm, for no particular reason. Nothing happened. I tried to move my left arm. Nothing happened. The same thing with my feet. I couldn't move them at all. I started to cry, and when I went to wipe the tears that were forming in puddles on my face, I couldn't move my arms.

Where am I? What's happening to me? Who's here?

93

They say that a person will always call for his mother when he's in trouble, and I was no different. I tried to call out.

"Ma . . . Ma . . . Ma . . ." I said over and over at the top of my voice. But the words never came out. Why?

"Tina . . . Tina . . . Tina . . ." I practically shouted at the top of my lungs. Still, the words were never heard. Then the lady in the white coat was standing over my bed, looking down.

"Don't try to talk," she said. "You can't talk because your mouth is full of plastic tubes that suck out the phlegm and keep you from choking to death. Those tubes up your nose are part of the respirator that's helping you breathe." She left the room.

I shut my eyes and started to cry again. It all began to come back. Jack Tatum had hit me on the football field. I couldn't get up right away. Now I was in a hospital. Something bad had happened to me. Something really bad. All these machines that were connected to me weren't hooked up for nothing. For what seemed an eternity, I was all alone, me and my thoughts. Why won't someone—anyone—come into this room and tell me what's wrong? Why? Why? Why? I didn't know what the hell was going on. I just knew I couldn't move—not a muscle. I just knew I had tubes in me everywhere. I thought that maybe I had just pinched a nerve, and that I'd be coming around in a day or two.

I didn't know I had been operated on the night before or that I had suffered a broken neck when Tatum hit me. I didn't know I was really lucky just to be alive. I certainly didn't know that barring a miracle, a real miracle, I would be a quadriplegic for the rest of my life, that I'd never be able to walk again or move any of the muscles from my neck down. I didn't know that I'd have to spend the rest of my days living either in a wheelchair or in a bed. I didn't know nuthin' about nuthin', as we used to say back in Chicago. I just knew that my body ached and pained all over, from head to toe.

Just then two doctors strolled into my room, looked down at me, talked quietly to one another, and then walked out. They weren't in my room for more than a minute. But why were they shaking their heads? Why were their faces so sad? Why couldn't they look me in the eye? Why were they in such a hurry to get out of my room? I had a lot of questions, but I couldn't ask them. And probably nobody wanted to answer them for me anyway.

Suddenly I heard more footsteps in my room, and there was a guy in a green coat standing over me. In his right hand he had what looked like a screwdriver. He's here to fix something, I thought. Maybe the air conditioner. Maybe the bed. Maybe the window.

"Hi," he said cheerfully.

I thought to myself, "This guy wouldn't be talking so happily if he couldn't move a muscle."

"I have some adjustments to make on your halo," he said. Halo? What halo? What the hell was he talking about?

"This big steel ring around your head is attached to an eighty-pound weight alongside your bed," he said. "The reason for it is to keep your head completely immobile." I didn't even know there was a halo around my head. "The halo is attached to your head with screws that have to be tightened twice a day. That's why I'm here. You'll be seeing a lot of me while you're here."

And then he took his screwdriver and went to work. "Don't be nervous," he said to me. "It only takes a couple of seconds to tighten 'em up." I was conscious of the pressure from the screwdriver tightening those screws into my head, and the pain—the incredible pain—not only in my head but over my entire body.

"Jesus Christ had to wear his crown of thorns," I said to myself, "and now I have to wear mine." Blood began to ooze out of my scalp and run into my eyes, down across my nose, and into my mouth. The more he tightened the screws, the more blood there was. He noticed I was in pain and was bothered by the blood in my eyes and my mouth, and in his own way he tried to calm me down.

"Ahh, that blood's nothing to worry about," he said. "It's quite normal. It'll stop in a minute or so, just bear with me." Bear with

95

him? What choice did I have? "Okay, that's it for now," he said, putting his screwdriver into the pocket of his green jacket. "Be back to see you again in a couple of hours." I couldn't wait. The guy made it sound as though he'd be making a social call, just dropping by for a visit.

A short time later a new nurse came into the room and stood over my bed. I was getting tired of having people look down on me all the time, but I had no other choice. I couldn't move my head.

"Time for lunch," she said, sounding almost as cheerful as the guy in the green coat with the screwdriver. That was the best news I'd heard since I woke up. All I wanted was a solid piece of bread. But my lunch came in a little plastic bag.

"Hold on just one second," the nurse said. She took the bag and connected it to something alongside my bed, and suddenly this white stuff started to come down a tube, twist and turn, and then disappear into my nose. That was lunch, intravenous style.

"It will fill you up for now," the nurse said. It did, too. When she came back to disconnect the intravenous tube, I felt as though I'd just had a nine-course meal at the Pump Room in Chicago, everything from shrimp cocktail to clam chowder to a thick, juicy steak to a double hot-fudge sundae.

I dozed off right after lunch, and when I woke up there was a hulking figure staring down at me. His eyes were red, and there were tears running down his cheeks. His hair was disheveled, the way it always was. I couldn't tell if his shirt was hangin' out, the way it always was. He held my hand and touched my face, the way a father would. It was John Madden, the head coach of the Oakland Raiders.

"Darryl, it'll be all right," he said to me, his voice so soft, so tender.

"Coach, what's the matter with me?" I tried to ask him. "Coach ... Coach ... Coach ... why won't they tell me what's wrong with me?" The coach kept shaking his head slowly from one side to the other.

Then, in a flash, John let go of my hand and started to wave his arms and yell, "Nurse! Nurse! Nurse!" It was just as if he was there on the sidelines in his black shirt and silver slacks and white shoes, screaming at an official—the John Madden people always saw on television. He was mad about something, but he also looked very worried. A nurse ran into my room, and Madden pointed to one of the machines alongside my bed.

"That's stopped!" Madden practically screamed to the nurse. "It was working when I came in here to see Darryl, but then it stopped. Just a minute ago. Fix the goddamned thing!"

Sure enough, a plug had come loose on the machine that was hooked up to the tubes in my mouth, and although I didn't know it, those tubes weren't suctioning the phlegm from my mouth the way they were supposed to. The nurse reconnected the tubes, and then she took a long suction tube, stuck it down my throat, and drew all the loose phlegm from my lungs. It hurt like crazy, and I started to cry. Why was this happening to me?

Thank God for the coach. I don't know how long he was with me because I kept dozing off and had no idea of the time. But if he hadn't been there and hadn't noticed that the suction tubes weren't working, I might have choked to death. Or at least that's what the nurse told me after he left to go back to the Raiders' training camp, which was more than an hour's drive away in Santa Rosa, California.

Madden hadn't been gone very long when I heard more footsteps in my room and saw still another face looking down at me. It was Tom Hoffman, the Patriots' business manager. Tom reached out and held my right hand, the way Coach Madden had. Suddenly Tom began to cry.

"Good God," I thought to myself, "everyone who's come to see me has cried. They're not crying just because I've got a muscle spasm. I must be in bad shape. Maybe I'm on my way out."

"I called Tina in Chicago this morning," Tom said, "and went over with her what happened in the game last night. I also had a prepaid ticket left for Tina and your mother at O'Hare Airport. Tina'll be here in a couple of hours, but I don't know when your mother's going to be out here. She's taken this pretty hard, and they probably won't let her travel for a couple of days."

Tom must've been told that I couldn't talk because of the tubes in my mouth, so he did all the talking, and I did all the listening.

He said that early in the first quarter of the Patriots-Raiders game, he had received a call from the ticket reservation window about two tickets I was supposed to have left for a couple of friends of mine from college who were working in the Bay Area and had called me the morning of the game looking for a pair of freebies. "I checked the comp list, Darryl," Tom said, "and didn't see your name in there for any tickets. So I ran down to the ticket window, talked to the two guys who were looking for the tickets in your name, convinced myself that they were really friends of yours and not just two guys using someone's name, and then arranged to get them into the game."

"Poor Tom," I thought. "He had to cover for me again. I had the worst habit of promising tickets to people and then forgetting to put their names on the ticket list."

Tom said, "Just when I got back to the press box, you got hit. Then at halftime, when you were on your way to the hospital, I had to leave the stadium and go to the Oakland Airport to check out all our arrangements for the charter flight back to Boston after the game. When I reached the operations office at the airport, I got a phone call from Jim Valek, who was back at the stadium. Jim told me that you had been badly hurt. He said he had already called Tina and told her that you had suffered a very serious injury. He told me to call Tina and make any arrangements that she and anybody else in your family needed to get out here."

All of a sudden Tom began to smile.

"You know what I had to do, Darryl? I had to crawl into the belly of the plane in my three-piece suit and sort through more than two hundred pieces of luggage to find my bags. It was hot as hell in there, and when I came out I was dripping with perspiration. I tried to find your bags, too, Darryl, but couldn't. Most of them didn't have any identification attached and I couldn't tell one from another.

"In case you didn't know, we won the game twenty-one to seven," Tom said. "But all the guys were down when they got to the airport. I think they had an idea that your injury was serious, and it took the edge off the victory. As the guys were getting on the plane, someone from operations came to get Chuck; there was a phone call for him.

"Chuck ran inside, and when he came back out he looked ten years older than he had just two minutes earlier. He went onto the plane, asked one of the stewardesses for the public address system, and then told the players he wanted their attention for a minute. He didn't even have to ask for it, Darryl. He said to the guys, 'That was John Madden who just called. He's been in touch with the doctors over at the hospital. Darryl's suffered a very grave injury. He needs all our prayers. Let's say a prayer for him right now. . . .'

"And Darryl, let me tell you, you could've heard a pin drop on that plane. I want you to know that everyone aboard that plane prayed for you. And everyone asked me to say hello to you and tell you that they haven't forgotten . . . and won't ever forget you."

The tears were rolling out of my eyes. Tom even had to take out his handkerchief to wipe off my face. I'd have done it myself, but I couldn't. Tom also told me that the Patriots' plane had a malfunction about a half-hour out of Oakland and had to turn back to make an emergency landing in San Francisco. "There was a lot of fuel leaking from one of the engines," he said, "and there were a dozen fire trucks alongside the runway when the pilot touched down. The guys had to wait there for five hours. Now they're back home safe."

Tom shook his head again. "Darryl," he said, "it was a bad night all around for the Patriots."

Just then another nurse came into the room, and I heard her tell Tom that he should be going, that he had been with me long enough, and that I wasn't in any condition to have guests for long periods. So Tom squeezed my hands, patted me on the face, and left the room. The nurse then gave me a shot of something—or at least she said she did; I never felt a thing—and I dozed off into another world.

Darryl Stingley continues to show some right-arm movement and some sensation over all parts of his body without significant change from this morning. Phone consultations have been carried out today with several neurosurgical and orthopedic experts throughout the country, and there was an examination by Dr. Glenn Reynolds, director of the California Regional Spinal Cord Injury Care System. All consultations recommend continuing present course of treatment with continuous spinal traction as well as close continuing care to general health. No further prognosis is possible at this time. He remains in intensive care for close observation.

**—Medical Bulletin No. 2, 6:00 P.M. PDT,
Sunday, August 13, 1978**

When I woke up, Tina was at my side, holding my hand, her face against mine. She was crying.

"Oh, Baby," she said over and over. "Oh, Baby . . . oh, Baby." She wore a look of shock, a look of hurt, a look of pain, a look of disbelief—all wrapped up into one. She looked seventy-five years old.

I wanted to talk to her, to ask her how she was, to ask her how our boys were, but the words wouldn't come out. So I just looked at her while she held my hand and smoothed her other hand across my face. It felt so good, I wanted her never to stop. Suddenly the peace and quiet of the room was interrupted by the guy in the green coat, who had come back to tighten each of the screws for the halo as deep into my head as they would go. The blood didn't ooze out this time. It poured out, runnng down into my eyes and across my nose and into my mouth or onto my chin. Tina couldn't stand the sight of blood, and she shut her eyes—and kept them shut.

"Okay, that does it for today," the man said, cheerful as ever. "I'll be back to see you first thing in the morning."

"Geez," I thought to myself, "I can't wait."

It was dinnertime, and the night nurse came in with another bag of liquid yuk, hitched it to my intravenous tubes, and turned on the feast. Oh, what I'd have given for a double order of ribs. Even a single order. This liquid stuff through the nose was for the birds. For dessert I got another shot—a sedative, I guessed—and in no time at all I was off in another world again.

Darryl Stingley, recovering from a cervical spine fracture/ dislocation injury, remains in good general condition in the intensive care unit under close observation. There has been little change in the condition of paralysis which began at the time of the injury, with some motion of the right arm and sensation to a limited degree over the entire body . . . to the same extent as yesterday.
—Medical Bulletin No. 3, 8:20 P.M. PDT,
Monday, August 14, 1978

My mother was at my bedside when I woke up Monday, and so was Tina. My mother was holding my left hand, Tina my right. I thought to myself, "They've got me where they always wanted me: right in the middle." Tina and my mother had not gotten along very well for some time, and I always found myself being sort of a referee when they had their little arguments.

My mother was a very nervous person and also suffered from hypertension. She was never at her best when things were at their

101

worst. Seeing me there in bed, with tubes in my nose and my mouth and a halo around my head, and knowing that I couldn't move, not even a muscle, was too much for her, and she broke down and cried. Tina tried to console her, but my mother was out of control. I wished she weren't in the room. She was making Tina upset. And she was making me upset. If only I could have talked to her. If only I could have told her to calm down, that I was going to be o.k. But I couldn't talk. And I didn't know if I was going to be all o.k. No one had told me a thing about my condition. Not a thing.

"I was at church when someone came and got me and told me that you'd been hurt in a football game," my mother said, sobbing. "I stayed in church and prayed to God that you'd be all right, that nothing bad would happen to you. And then when I went home, as I walked into the apartment that picture of you on the living room wall—the one where you're wearing your Patriots red-and-white uniform—fell off the wall and shattered into a million pieces. It took me an hour to clean up all the glass."

My mother would have gone on forever, but my friend in the green coat came by to do his thing and Tina suggested to my mother that what the guy was going to do to me would be too much for her. She told my mother how I'd start to bleed and, well, that was all my mother had to hear. "Good-bye for now," she said, wiping some more tears from her eyes. "I'm going to the chaplain's office to pray for you and ask him to take care of you. I'll be there praying if you need me."

Tina stayed with me throughout the day, never leaving my bedside, never taking her hand away from mine. She was quiet for long stretches. I could understand her mood, and I only wished I could have spoken to her. I think I could have made her feel a whole lot better than she obviously was feeling. A month or so ago she had seen her man leave his home in Chicago and go off to work in New England as healthy a person as you could ever find. Now that same man was flat on his back, unable to talk, unable to move, unable to do anything for himself. It was a tough thing for her to handle.

All day long one doctor after another, and one nurse after another, came into my room to check me out. They were mostly nameless and faceless people to me, because I never saw half of them. They'd come in, play around with the machines or the tubes, touch various parts of my body, read their charts, and then they'd be gone, just like that. The only nurse I liked was the one who came by to give me my shot of painkiller a couple of times a day. When the shot wore off, the pain would be unbearable, and it would show on my face.

"Stop making faces," Tina said to me that night after my usual dinner of intravenous glop.

I started to cry. I didn't know I was making faces. I didn't want to make faces. But I couldn't stand the pain that had spread over my entire body, from head to toe. And because of the tubes in my mouth I couldn't tell anyone how much I was hurting. While I was still crying, a whole team of doctors and nurses entered my room. There were enough people around my bed to play a football game.

"Just going to take some X rays," one of the doctors said. So they took all their pictures, dozens of them—thank God no one told me to smile for the camera—and then one of the nurses gave me another shot. It was amazing how they gave me those shots. "Mr. Stingley, this won't hurt a bit," a voice would say. And it never would hurt. I was getting so many shots, though, that I began to think that my skin must look like one of those connect-the-dots games for little kids. In a matter of moments I was out.

Darryl Stingley spent a restful night Monday following X-ray diagnostic tests to determine the need for surgery. The tests indicated no need for surgery at this time, and he will remain under close observation, continuing in the spinal traction begun the night of the injury. The condition of

paralysis remains unchanged. Doctors note that at least ten to fourteen days will have to elapse before a meaningful estimation of recovery prognosis can be made.
> **—Medical Bulletin No. 4, 8:00 A.M. PDT,**
> **Tuesday, August 15, 1978**

Someone was holding my hand when I woke up Tuesday, and I knew it wasn't Tina. Her hands were a lady's hands, small and somewhat soft. These hands belonged to a workingman, someone who had used his hands to make a living, because they were big and hard and calloused. They belonged to my father, who had flown out the night before with my brother Wayne.

My father was crying, and I started to cry, too. At this moment he probably wanted to be strong and reassuring and supportive—a father, in other words—but the emotion of the scene, of seeing his son in bed with that halo was too much for him.

"My baby, my baby, my baby . . ." he said over and over. "What did they do to my baby? Why? Why did this have to happen to you?" He couldn't talk for several minutes, and finally he had to take out his handkerchief and wipe away his tears. And mine. He tightened his grip on my hand.

"Darryl, you know how us Stingleys are," he said. "They may try to count us out, but we're never out. Darryl, you can't keep a Stingley down. We're going to tough this thing out and fight it, and you're gonna be o.k." And then my father was lost for words. Wayne sat by my bed and tried to talk to me, but he couldn't make much sense. He knew that he had been my idol when I was a kid and that I had tried to follow in his footsteps at Marshall High. I'm sure he was probably saying to himself, "I wish I had never played football, because then Darryl wouldn't be where he is right now."

While my father and Wayne were in the room, the man in the green coat stopped by for his regular morning visit. I now thought of him as a mechanic and nothing else, and I couldn't stand the sight of him. I knew he was there to help me, but I also knew that when he showed up I'd be suffering even greater pain for a few minutes—and shedding blood. Tina told my father and Wayne that it would be best for them if they left for a few minutes, and they did.

When the mechanic was finished fixing my head, I had another visitor: John Madden. The coach said he'd been in to see me the day before, too, but that I was asleep and the nurses didn't want to wake me. Just seeing the coach helped make my day.

"You're lookin' better," he said. Maybe I was, I didn't know. I sure wasn't feelin' any better, though. "The guys on the Raiders all said to say hello and that they're wishin' you a speedy recovery."

I sure appreciated the coach telling me that, but in the back of my head I really couldn't believe that Jack Tatum had sent his best wishes to me. The other Raiders, yes. Tatum, no. Tatum, as best as I could tell, didn't have feelings for anyone except Jack Tatum.

The coach told me some things that were happening around the NFL. He mentioned the names of some players who'd been cut, but none of the names rang a bell. He told me that the Raiders weren't playing very well, that he didn't think the team was as good as all the experts thought. I got the feeling from listening to him that it was going to be a long season for the Raiders. After Madden left, I dozed off, and when I awoke, Tina said to me, "Baby, you just took a six-hour nap." You could have fooled me.

Darryl Stingley's condition has improved slightly since the time of his admission. He was originally without movement or feeling in the arms or legs or trunk of his body. Following successful reduction of the dislocation immediately following the accident, he began to improve. Mr. Stingley has regained sensation through all parts of the body but there has been no return of movement except to a limited but gratifying degree in his right arm. He remains in tong traction in a special circular orthopedic bed. A myelograph-

ic exam performed on Monday revealed there is no pressure on the spinal cord. His prognosis is uncertain, although
some degree of cautious optimism seems warranted at this
time.

—Medical Bulletin No. 5, 4:30 P.M. PDT,
Tuesday, August 15, 1978

The days passed into nights and the nights passed into days.
Lying in this bed, I lost all track of time, of where I was. I couldn't
move my head because of the infernal steel halo and the eighty-
pound weight to which it was attached. I had tubes in my mouth. I
was fed through my nose. I was getting shots all over the place. I
couldn't talk. I couldn't move my arms or my legs. I couldn't move
anything. I was totally helpless.

In those early days in the hospital all my communication was
done with my eyes. I inspected everything going on; that is,
everything I was able to see from my stabilized position in bed. I
tried—desperately tried—to read the expressions on the faces of
the doctors and the nurses, and also on the faces of my family, to
try to get an idea of the severity of my condition. The doctors
always seemed to be whispering to one another, same with the
nurses. It didn't take long to figure out that when the doctors and
nurses were whispering to one another, the patient was in trouble. When they stopped whispering, I could tell from the looks on
their faces that my situation wasn't exactly a piece of cake. It was
grave. Really grave.

For long periods of time I was connected to a respirator
machine, and if anyone even got close to the respirator, my eyes
would light up and my face would tense. Get away from me! Get
away from me! I couldn't say those things myself because of the
tubes in my mouth, but I wanted to shout them at the top of my
lungs. I was scared that someone would pull the plug, that the
respirator would be disconnected accidentally, and that I wouldn't
be able to breathe on my own. Maybe it was a natural reaction,

maybe it wasn't, but I became frightened of almost everyone who came into that room except the members of my family, John Madden, and Tom Hoffman, who was like a brother to me because he was always on call to do anything and everything for all of us.

God, was I paranoid with everyone else. Don't pull the plug! Don't! Get the hell out of here, you s.o.b.'s! My eyes said it all. Unplug that respirator and . . . I'd be moving on.

I felt that certain nurses were definitely out to get me. One nurse came in a couple of times a day to adjust my oxygen intake. How did I know she was helping me? I had it in my mind that she was trying to get rid of me, that she was trying to cut off my life-support system. I kept thinking, "This dumb nurse couldn't care less if Darryl Stingley goes out of this hospital in a long box." All I knew is that the oxygen machine was helping keep me alive, and she was messing with it. My eyes told her that I hated her, and I hoped she got the message. All I ever wanted her to do was get the hell out of my room and stop screwing around with my life. Tina could tell from the look in my eyes that I was suspicious of all these creeps, and she was always trying to calm me down and soothe my fears.

"Baby, the nurses are just following orders," she'd say. "I've talked to them to find out what they're doing, and what they're doing is trying to get you to do as much as you can for yourself. The more breathing you can do for yourself, the better it is for you. They want you to reach the point where you won't need any respirator machine." I didn't believe her. No way. Those people all were out to do away with me.

I really had it in for one doctor, a young guy, because he always made me feel that I was on my way out. He was never encouraging. His bedside manner was, you might say, crude. Most doctors wear a smile when they come into your room, even if they know you're on the way out. Not this dude. He'd come in, his face would be sad, and he'd look at me, look at my charts, check my vital signs . . . and then I'd detect his head shaking, as if he were saying,

"This guy's not going to make it out of here. Too bad." I thought of him as "the Devil." I'd have called him the Devil to his face if I could. He was a demon, the most negative thing I could think of, and he represented the worst: Death. Just lying there watching him day in and day out, I developed this terrible fear of him: He was the negative impulse of my situation, the worst thing imaginable. That dude gave me hallucinations.

One doctor I really did like. His name, I found out, was Dr. Francis Johnson. He understood me. He was never gloomy, and his bedside manner was to be encouraging. He'd come by and look at my charts and say, "Hey, Darryl, you're doin' better. We'll probably be able to send you home soon." He may not have believed a word of what he told me, particularly the part about sending me home soon, and I didn't believe a word of what he said, but here I was struggling to survive, fighting for my life, and he was encouraging me. It made my day when Dr. Johnson came around.

All this time everything in my life was changing radically. I had to find a way to cope, to continue living. I had to develop an ability to adjust to the obstacles that presented themselves. I was in a totally adverse environment, and the only way to approach it was to try to make as many adjustments as necessary to survive, to function, to communicate. I had no choice. It was up to me.

After four or five days in the hospital, I realized I was paralyzed, and that I probably wouldn't be walking out of the hospital any day soon—if ever. No one told me that. They didn't have to. I still couldn't move a muscle. My whole body was virtually useless. I wasn't stupid. I had a pretty good idea of what was happening to me, and what had happened to me.

The knowledge was with me all the time, but I tried to keep it out of my mind as much as possible, because when I thought about it, I cried. And when I cried, my family cried too. I had to be strong. I had to stand up and be counted and show everyone—the doctors, the nurses, my family—that I was up to the fight ahead. I couldn't be any other way.

As time passed, I became more aware of my surroundings and of what was happening to me. My bed, I was told, was something called a Stryker Frame. I called it the "Pancake." I was strapped flat on my back in the bed, so the doctors and the nurses could flip the Pancake whichever way they wanted—and me along with it. When they'd want to get my blood circulating in some other way, they'd just turn me over or onto my side or straight up and down. One night when I was asleep they turned me all the way over so that I was face down to the floor, and when I woke up there was Tina stretched out underneath me on the floor, her face practically nose to nose with mine. She kissed me.

"Baby, I'm here to read you the sports pages," she said, smiling. "I'll bet you never got such good service as this before." She sure was right about that. I hadn't.

My room at Eden Hospital wasn't exactly a lavish suite at the Ritz, at least from what I could tell from my various positions aboard the Pancake. I was in the intensive-care unit, the I.C.; it was a miniward, with a half dozen beds in the main area plus two small private chambers. In the center of the big room were desks where the I.C. nurses did their work when they weren't at one of the patients' bedside. The set-up at the nurses' station looked like something out of the 22nd century; there were machines and screens and consoles everywhere, all relaying data on each of the patients in the I.C. One of the nurses always kept her eyes glued to those screens and machines. It was easy to tell when something was amiss because the nurses would all start scrambling around and doctors would suddenly be coming out of the woodwork. There were few dull moments in the I.C.

I was in one of the private chambers, which came complete with a wash basin in the corner, soundproof tiles on the ceiling (so a person's screams couldn't be heard all over the hospital, I guessed), a light in the overhead panel, a small bedside table, and a mini-television set that could be swung into any position I wanted.

Watching TV was not easy to do, so I didn't watch much of it. I was given a pair of prism glasses by one of the nurses. They were like a refractive triangle. I was strapped to the bed on my back, and when I looked through the glasses as I lay on my back, I'd see the picture from the TV set over in the corner of the room. It may sound simple, but it sure got confusing at times. I'd think I was looking at the ceiling, but I'd be seeing the TV screen.

I tried not to watch football, because I didn't want to be reminded of what had happened to me. Seeing people beat up on one another would have done that. Besides, I wasn't into football. I was into me. Into living. I caught some of the news shows and the lighter comedy stuff at night. I figured that the more I laughed, the better off I'd be.

Most of the space in my room was taken up by a chair in the corner across from the entrance—some member of my family was always in that chair, awake or asleep—and by all these machines and consoles with dozens of buttons and switches and screens on them.

When I was first brought into the room, the walls were bare. No pictures. No nothing.

"This place is like a prison," I thought one day when I was flipped around on the Pancake and got a look at my new home. But before a week or so was out, those same walls were plastered with get-well cards and telegrams from people all over the country, in football and out of football, and there were flower arrangements all over the place. Tina read each and every card and telegram to me. There were a lot of cards from the New York Jets. It seemed like I got a get-well-quick card from every Jet player, every coach, everyone in their front office. All I knew about the Jets before was that they were in our division and we were supposed to have a dislike for them. But I gained tremendous respect and admiration for them as individuals because they all took the time to show they cared. In fact, I received so many cards and flowers that one day I sent a whole cartful of plants and flowers upstairs to the Oakland Raiders' private hospital room where, I was told, Rod Martin, a linebacker, was recovering from knee surgery.

The nurses' station was in the center of the I.C., exactly four paces from the door to my room. I knew it was exactly four paces because I counted the footsteps every time I knew the nurse would be coming to see me, to give me a shot or my yuk or whatever. Outside the door to the I.C. was the office of the chaplain, Les Meltzer. He said he was nondenominational, the man for everyone. We took him at his word: The Stingley clan just about took over his office, and Tom Hoffman established his headquarters there.

After five or six days, my father had gone back to Chicago because he couldn't afford to be away from his job, but Tina, my mother, and my brother Wayne were all still with me. Thanks to the Patriots, they all had rooms at a nearby hotel. But those rooms didn't get much use. I don't think Tina ever used hers. She slept alongside me in the bed or in the chair in the corner every night. My mother went to the hotel only to sleep. As for Wayne, he'd visit me for a little while every day and then go on over to San Francisco to check out the action. I really couldn't blame him, either. If I had been in his shoes, I'd have been doing the same thing.

One day Tom Hoffman asked me if it would be O.K. for what he called a pool photographer to come into the I.C. and take some pictures of me that would be wired to all the newspapers and magazines in the country. Tom told me he had been swamped with requests from the media for interviews and photos, and that this one picture session might be the best way to keep everyone happy. I could understand his problem, but I didn't want anyone taking any pictures of me. I couldn't even look at myself in the mirror, I was so ugly. I had all these tubes sticking out everywhere, and my head looked like a battleground. I didn't want anyone to see me that way. Tom got the message from the look in my eyes.

"I understand," he said. "We'll let them come in here when you feel good about yourself."

On the whole, I thought I was making pretty good progress, at least it seemed like progress, after my first ten days. I still couldn't talk. I couldn't move a muscle. And that damn halo was still around my head. But I had periods when the pain throughout my body wasn't as bad as it had been just a second or two before, and in my own mind I read this as progress.

During my first ten or twelve days in the hospital I had only a few visitors each day: Tina, who never left; my mother, who was so wound up about my condition that she could only stay in the room for a couple of minutes at a time; my brother Wayne, who always had some new stories about his experiences the previous night in San Francisco; Tom Hoffman, who read me the football news and the player cuts each day; and the Maddens, John and his wife, Virginia.

I missed many of the Coach's visits because I was either sleeping or with the doctors, but John came by to see me just about every day. Once he arrived in my room close to midnight and apologized for being so late. I wasn't even expecting him. The Raiders had played a game that day in Denver, and when their plane landed back in Oakland, John rushed right over to see me. I can't tell you the love I have for that man. Here he was trying to get his football team ready for the new season in a training camp more than an hour's drive away, yet he still found time to come to the hospital each day to try to cheer me up. And Virginia was forever stopping by or calling or doing things to help my family. One night she even had my family over to her house for dinner.

John and I never talked about serious things, or my injury. We just shot the breeze. He'd be telling me about his team, about who was looking good and who wasn't looking good, and I'd take it all in. Because of my accident, I got to see a side of John Madden I had never known existed. Maybe the people in Oakland knew what a warm and loving and compassionate man he was, but I doubt that many other people around the country knew it.

John resigned as coach of the Raiders after that 1978 season. He was only in his early forties but he said his ulcers couldn't take the pressure of NFL coaching—of having to win—any longer. Maybe they couldn't. But I suspect that my accident, and the condition it left me in, had something to do with his decision to leave the sidelines. I think that the thought of my lying there on my pancake—helpless, motionless—affected him deeply.

When John announced his retirement, he told a story about himself that, he said, reflected exactly how much the game of football had consumed him over the years. Over dinner one night Virginia apparently said to him, "We're going to think about getting a car for Mike." John just smiled and said, "Yeah, that's right. He'll be old enough to get his license in three or four years." Virginia was practically speechless.

"John," she said, "our son is sixteen years old, and you can drive a car when you're sixteen."

As John told the story, he said that he had so devoted himself to football—twenty-four hours a day, seven days a week, fifty-two weeks a year—that he had not taken the time to see Mike or his younger son, Joe grow up. "I'm quitting so I can spend some time with my kids," John said.

Early one morning while Tina was reading me the paper, a couple of orderlies walked into my room, played around with some screws on my bed, and suddenly I was being wheeled out of the I.C. and down some corridors leading into a cold room. Poor Tina didn't know what was going on—and neither did I.

"We're just going to do a myelogram on you, Mr. Stingley," said a doctor I'd never seen before. A myelogram? What the hell was a myelogram? Nobody ever told me anything.

"The good news is that we won't have to transfer you to this swivel-type top, because your Stryker Frame is essentially the same thing," the doctor said when I was wheeled into what looked like a mini–operating room. If that was the good news, I wanted to know the bad news. Nobody told me. I learned for myself.

"All right, Mr. Stingley," the doctor said, "I'm going to inject this dye into your spinal column." So far, so good. Then the pain began. God, did it hurt.

"Now, Mr. Stingley, I'm going to turn your frame every which way and we're going to float the dye up and down your spinal column to find out, or double-check, exactly where it is that the discs and the vertebrae are out of whack. I know the pain you're feeling, but just bear with us for a little while." God, it hurt. Did it ever hurt.

Two or three times they actually drained the fluid from my head—and it felt as though it was going to fall off. I was in never-never land.

"Normally, Mr. Stingley, patients getting a myelogram can see the fluid running up and down their spinal column by looking at that screen over there, but you won't be able to see anything because you can't move your head," the doctor said. No kidding, Dick Tracy. And then, at last, it was over. It took about forty-five minutes to do, and all I can say is this: A myelogram is the world's worst torture. Never sign up for one unless you've got the highest tolerance for pain in the entire world.

"Thank you, Mr. Stingley," the doctor said. "We've learned what we had to learn."

As I was being wheeled out of the room, another doctor said to me, "Mr. Stingley, whatever you do, don't move your head for the next forty-eight hours or else you'll get terrible headaches for a couple of weeks." Was this guy for real? I didn't know whether he was being sarcastic or being a comedian. You try moving your head when you're flat on your back with an eighty-pound weight attached to a halo that's screwed into your scalp. I sure didn't move, but you know what? I still got the headaches. Some people just can't win.

A spinal stabilization procedure has been scheduled for Darryl Stingley and will be performed on Wednesday morning, August 23, at Eden Hospital by Dr. Manard Pont, Mr. Stingley's attending neurosurgeon, and his associates. Dr. Ronald Birkenfeld of Boston, the New England Patriots' consulting neurosurgeon, will be present at the time of surgery.
—Medical Bulletin No. 6, 4:00 P.M. PDT, Tuesday, August 22, 1978

Back in my room that night, I kept thinking about what that one doctor had said: "We've learned what we had to learn." What was it they had to learn? I found out soon enough, when Dr. Pont and Dr. Birkenfeld came into my room.

"Darryl," Dr. Pont said, "we're going to operate on you again tomorrow. We're going to fuse a couple of the vertebrae in your neck because we want to fully secure it. We have no reason to believe that this operation will be anything less than one hundred percent successful." There wasn't much for me to say because I couldn't talk anyway. The next morning two orderlies came and wheeled me down into the operating room.

Darryl Stingley underwent surgery this morning. A spinal fusion of the fourth and fifth cervical vertebrae was performed during the procedure in order to stabilize his neck. The operation and the anesthesia were uneventful, and a highly satisfactory bone position was obtained. His postoperative condition is excellent.
—Medical Bulletin No. 7, 6:00 P.M. PDT, Wednesday, August 23, 1978

115

When I woke up from the anesthesia, Tina was right beside me, as always, holding my hand.

"Everything went just fine," she said, and I wanted to believe her. All day, every day, Tina did her best to convince me I'd be O.K., that I was getting better and better all the time. The problem was, I knew I still couldn't move my legs or my arms or anything else, and I was still wearing a halo around my head. Maybe I was improving, but aside from the occasional—and so brief—moments of reduced pain I had no reason to think so.

Communicating such thoughts to other people was, in a word, a bitch. After all, I simply couldn't talk. It was a few days after I came out of that spinal-fusion surgery that two nurses or therapists—at that point I couldn't tell one from the other—came into my room carrying a stack of boards and said to me, "Darryl, we're gonna teach you a whole new way to talk."

"What's this?" I thought, "Ned and the third-grade reader?"

"All right, Darryl," one of the ladies in white said, "we'll start with this board right here." On that board were the names of people in my family and also Tom Hoffman's name.

"When you want to speak to someone," the lady said, "we'll just run our fingers down the list, Tina to Mother to Wayne to Tom Hoffman, and all you have to do is blink when we come to the name of the person you want to talk to. Then we'll get that person, and you can have your conversation." Having a conversation was another story in itself.

"Now, when you want to talk to this other person, they can use this board here," the lady said, producing a board that had all the letters of the alphabet on it and numbers from 1 to 10. "You know how to spell Darryl," the lady said. "All the other person has to do is point to the letters, and when they come to the one you want, just blink. That's your signal. Let's say you want to ask Tina, 'How are the boys?' Tina'll just start working the alphabet. When she reaches the H, you blink. Then the O, then the W, and so on until it all comes out. You'll find that Tina and the others will catch the drift of your questions long before you have to spell them all out. It's complicated, we know. But it's the best thing for you until they remove the tubes from your mouth and throat. So let's not condemn it. Let's give it a try." I was ready to try anything.

When Tina returned to the room, I was all set to play my new game. She picked up the alphabet board, and then she started right from the letter A.

"You want an A?" she said, smiling. I didn't blink. "How about a B?" Still no blinking.

It took ten minutes, but I finally got my question across: How're my boys?

Tina looked like she was ready to cry when she understood my question.

"Hank and Derek are great," she said. Ever since she'd arrived at the hospital, she'd been telling me how great they were, and just hearing their names helped make my day. "They're getting ready to go back to school and just waiting to see you again."

Just waiting to see you again.

Those words hit me hard. Tina could see it in my eyes. I was hurting suddenly. I wanted to see my boys, too. More than anything else in the world, I wanted to see them. But I couldn't let them see me now. I was not the father they remembered. I was confined to a bed, and probably would never walk again. And I had this monstrous halo around my head. Yes, my boys would see me again. But, dammit, not before that halo was gone from my head. I couldn't let them see me with that still on. I just couldn't.

Tina must have read in my eyes the anguish I was going through, because she took my hand and said to me, "Darryl, I understand. I understand completely. But the time will come, and it will be a great day for all of us."

Now that I had had the fusion surgery, the doctors relaxed the rules about visits, and suddenly everybody and their brother seemed to be coming through the walls. Several of the Oakland players visited me as often as they could.

No, Jack Tatum never came by. Not once. In his book, Tatum claimed he tried to reach me. Right. I was easy to reach because I couldn't go anywhere. And no message ever got to me saying Tatum had called.

One day Mike McCoy and Dave Rowe, a couple of defensive linemen, drove down from camp in Santa Rosa, and it didn't take them long to put everyone in the room into hysterics. Rowe strolled into the room, a big hulking figure, pulled the covers off my legs, shook his head and said, "Say, have there been some rustlers in here?"

My mother looked confused. "No . . . of course not."

"Hmm," Rowe said, "well somebody sure stole Darryl's calves."

They had, indeed. I had been about 195 pounds the night I played against the Raiders three or so weeks earlier, and now I was down to about 160.

Chuck Fairbanks and his wife, Puddy, flew out from New England for a very brief visit and then flew right back home. "We all miss you," Chuck said, "and we're just waiting for you to come back."

I was hoping he'd say, "We're saving your place in the starting lineup for you." But I guess I was too much of a dreamer. Then he talked to me about the team. "Practice has been a downer, Darryl," he said. "I think the guys still have your accident on their minds." I could understand that. I know if I had seen one of my teammates wiped out, I'd have had a hard time getting it out of my mind.

"We come back here to Oakland to play the Raiders on September twenty-fourth," Fairbanks said. "We're all going to come up and see you after the game. And we're going to bring you a nice present. The game ball."

Billy Sullivan, the owner of the Patriots, was a visitor one afternoon, too, but I was having a bad time of it that day and never really knew he was there. I got a real surprise another day when Ray Perkins stopped in. After Sam Rutigliano left, Perk had been the receivers' coach in New England but had moved on to San Diego for a job as the Chargers' offensive coordinator. The Chargers had an off day, and Perk came from San Diego to Oakland to cheer me up. When he came in, I was upside down on my Pancake. "We can't keep meeting this way, Darryl," he said.

Perk's another one of those guys who's supposed to be cold and calculating, a robot, no fun to be with. Maybe he's that way on the surface, but deep down he's warm and a good friend to have. (Perkins became head coach of the New York Giants in 1979, but resigned from the Giants after the 1982 season when Bear Bryant personally selected Perk to succeed him as head coach at Alabama; not long after Perk took over, the Bear died.) "They'll have you out of here soon, Darryl," Perk said as he left.

I didn't know about that because just when I'd think the pain seemed to be getting less, suddenly I'd have a bad period and it would be worse than ever. I could never predict the pain. To varying degrees it was always there. Always.

Still, I thought I was making progress, and that, as the doctors and nurses were always telling me, was the important thing.

Then, a week or so after the spinal fusion operation, the Devil came by on his regular call. He wore his usual sad face. One look at him, and I was ready to order up my casket. This time he put the stethoscope on my chest, listened for a few seconds, then stood back and looked really serious. I read the worst, the absolute worst, in his face. He turned and walked out. Within moments my room was filled with doctors and nurses, all whispering to one another. "They're having their annual medical convention," I thought.

What I didn't know then, and what they weren't telling me, was that one of my lungs had collapsed and I had developed pneumonia.

During the past three days there have been significant problems and complications regarding Darryl Stingley's

lungs. These problems, despite vigorous treatment, persist and are potentially life threatening. During this period the pulmonary problems have been treated by Darryl's attending physicians—Dr. Manard Pont, neurosurgeon; Dr. Donald Fink, Oakland Raiders team physician; Dr. Wing Chin, internal medicine specialist; Dr. Francis Johnson, medical director of pulmonary care; Dr. Robert Merwin, cardiologist; Dr. Robert Ecker, chest surgeon; and Dr. Steven Oppenheimer, specialist in infectious disease problems. Darryl Stingley's condition is now considered SERIOUS. His family remains with him constantly. Darryl, his family and his physicians remain grateful for the many prayers and the concern of Darryl's friends and fans.

—Medical Bulletin No. 8, 11:00 A.M., PDT,
Friday, September 1, 1978

That night Dr. Pont told me about the collapsed lung and the pneumonia. He didn't tell me that my condition was officially listed as serious. I didn't feel that bad, really. I was still on the respirator so I was breathing without too much difficulty. I still had the trach down my throat, too, and the phlegm was being sucked out by the gob.

But the doctors could tell from what they read on my machines that I wasn't as healthy as I felt. Not by a long shot. Now that the lung had collapsed, they were afraid that my chest would go next. And that would be all she wrote.

A couple of days earlier my Grannie Annie—Anna Brown, my mother's mother—had come out from Chicago to see me. She has a deep religous background, and has always been like a rock, a stabilizing force, when things weren't going well in the family. After Dr. Pont left the room, I felt the need for prayer—and plenty of it. I felt the need for Grannie Annie. Tina read the concern in my eyes, but didn't know what I wanted.

"A doctor?" she asked. I didn't blink. "A nurse?" Still no

blinking. "Your mother?" Nothing. "Wayne? No... Grannie Annie?"

I blinked my eyes several times.

Dr. Chin was still in my room, and when he saw me blink after Tina mentioned my Grannie Annie, he said, "Darryl wants his grandmother. Go get her and bring her here."

She was just in the chaplain's office, a couple of dozen steps away, and so she arrived as quick as you could say Grannie Annie. She had brought some blessed oil with her from Chicago, and she had it with her now. She rubbed it over me, rubbed it all over my body and my head.

"This is God's own oil," she said. "It will make you well." And she rubbed some more. "Darryl," she said, "I'm goin' to fast until your pneumonia is gone, till you're back on your feet again."

"No, don't do that, Grannie," Tina said.

"Okay, I'll just keep prayin' every minute," she said. And she did. She never stopped.

The gravity of my situation really hit me a few moments later when Wayne came back into my room. Wayne was usually happy-go-lucky when he came to see me. "How ya doin', little brother?" he'd say, breaking into a big smile. "Let me tell you what happened over in Frisco last night." Now he was acting strange. Very strange. He didn't tell me about the day's happenings in the world of sports, as he always did. He didn't crack any jokes or tell me stories of his activities in San Francisco. Instead, he was very quiet, not saying a word, just looking at me and trying to hold back tears. He wore a sour expression on his face, one I had never seen on him. And he looked like someone who had lost his best friend.

He wasn't the Wayne Stingley that I knew. There was a long silence, and suddenly Wayne said very slowly: "I'm gonna stay here with you all night tonight." I looked puzzled. "Yep, I'm gonna stay right by your side all night. I'm not goin' nowhere."

I looked up at him again, and he put his head down and rested it on the side of my bed. Right then I said to myself, "Something's wrong." I knew Wayne well enough to know he was reacting to something going on, something that had to be bad. And he wasn't going to tell me what it was. Was it me? Was something wrong with Tina? She had left my room a few minutes before Wayne came in. Was she O.K.? What was wrong? Tell me—please!

Just then Tina walked back into the room, came to the side of my bed, and grabbed my hand. "I'm not going anywhere the rest of the night," she said. "I'm stayin' here with you." Tina stayed with me in the room on most nights, and never told me in advance that she was staying. Why was she telling me now? What was up? Dammit, what was happening?

Suddenly, I broke down and cried, and then Tina and Wayne joined in. I didn't know it, but one of the doctors had called my family together in the chaplain's office while my Grannie Annie was in my room.

"I'm very sorry," he told Tina, my mother and Wayne, "but Darryl's probably not going to make it through the night. He has pneumonia bad, and because of his collapsed lung, his breathing is a problem for him. Unfortunately, there are no good signs present to make us think he'll pull through." Now, with Tina and Wayne at my bed, I stopped crying. I looked at Wayne, who reminded me of a wet dog. He was never a good actor, and he certainly couldn't mask his grief. Neither, for that matter, could Tina.

"I'm not goin' nowhere tonight," Wayne kept saying over and over. "I'm stayin' right here next to you."

Then my mother came into my room, a wreck, as usual. She was always nervous and jittery when she was around me in the hospital, which was why I didn't like her to be there for too long. Now she was so nervous, so jittery, so uptight, that no one in the family could stand it. "Geez, just looking at her makes me think I'm on my way out," I thought. "She sure isn't very encouraging." All she was doing, of course, was reacting in her own way to the message the doctor had just given her, but I didn't know that.

"My son, we are praying for you," she said, crying. "We are asking Him to look after you, and we know He will answer our prayers." Now she couldn't control her tears. "I'm goin' to the chaplain's office, and I'll be there if you need me." And she was gone.

I was really scared, more scared than I had ever been. I could think only one thing, that the worst was coming. Death. I wasn't afraid of dying. If it had to be, it had to be. I could reconcile myself to death. I could accept it. But I still wanted to live. I wanted to see my boys grow. I wanted to play catch with them again and kick a football around. Regardless of the way they had come into this world, they were my pride and joy . . . and I couldn't imagine their lives without me. Or my life without them.

And so I closed my eyes. Right away I began to entertain thoughts of death. My death. I had this dream over and over. I was in a casket and I saw people coming by the casket. It was my casket, and they were crying. I saw Tina. I saw my mother. Grannie Annie. My father. My boys, Hank and Derek, all dressed in neat little suits. My brothers, Harold and Wayne. My sister, Andrea. I saw some of my old teammates, Russ Francis, Sam Cunningham and Leon Gray, Prentice McCray. Chuck Fairbanks was there and so was Ray Perkins. John Madden was there with his wife, Virginia . . . everyone. That dream passed, thank God, and then I said to myself, "Darryl, once again you've got to call on that source of strength you've been calling on for so long. It's that time again."

Tina was next to me on the bed, Wayne was sitting in the chair now, and a nurse was looking over at me. But I felt all alone in the room. I asked my God, "Please don't forsake me now." Over and over, I asked Him not to forsake me. I made no outlandish promises. I didn't tell Him that I'd do this or I'd do that if He gave me my life. I just prayed and prayed, until I couldn't pray any more.

"If I am to die, then Your will is done," I said to Him. "It is my

123

wish at this time to live. Wherever I am when I wake will be all right with me. Wherever I am, it will be Your will, and I'm not arguing with You. If I have to go, I have to go. If You want me now, take me. But I pray that You spare me . . . for now."

Those were my last words, my last thoughts, and I felt sort of relieved as I passed into sleep. I had asked for my God's will to be done, that's all. There was nothing else I could do. I was in His hands.

The next thing I knew, it was morning. Tina was alongside me, still asleep. Wayne was out of it in the chair. One by one the doctors and nurses came into the room to look at me. I got the feeling from looking at them that they expected me to be cold as a cucumber. But there I was in living and breathing color. Alive, not dead. Thank you, God.

Dr. Pont came into the room, and his reaction was, like, "Hey, good God, Darryl's still alive!"

My family was ecstatic.

"Hey, Babes, what a great day," Tina said, wiping back her tears.

Wayne said, "Tonight, Brother, I'm going over to Frisco and really celebrate."

My mother was all gushy and crying, and my Grannie Annie was still praying away a mile a minute. Their man had pulled through.

From that day on—Saturday, September 2, 1978—everything got better. Each morning the therapists would come in and work me hard; before then, they had just sort of given me the once-over-lightly treatment. Now, they'd take my arms and legs and work them in different directions, to try to get some movement and circulation going. It hurt, really hurt at times, but the pain of the therapy didn't bother me. I had been to hell and back, or at least that's the way I looked at it, and nothing could stop me now. Nothing.

After a few more days the pneumonia was under control and my lungs were clear, so for the first time since I entered the hospital on August 12, the tubes were removed from my nose and my mouth. I could eat certain normal foods. No more yuk! No more blinking signals!

I could eat . . . and I could talk.

"Wayne," I said to my brother, "I'd like you to do me a favor tonight when you're over in San Francisco. Go down to the wharf, to one of those fish places, and get me the biggest takeout order of New England clam chowder you can find. Bring it back here and we'll have a feast. That's all I want: a lot of New England clam chowder."

My brother laughed. "This one," he said, "will be on me."

As my condition continued to improve, I still looked like a basket case, with my weight down below 150 pounds, but I was alive and well—and not complaining. Dr. Pont stopped by on one of his daily calls, and I said to him, "Doc, I have just one favor to ask. Will you please take this damn halo off my head?"

"Sorry, Darryl," he said, "but that's the one thing we can't do yet. We're going to keep you here for about another month, to monitor your progress. You're going to get colds, and we'll want to keep them in check. And we want that neck of yours to stabilize and get strong. You'll have that halo for another ten or twelve weeks. We can't risk taking it off now, not after all you've been through. The neck is a very delicate part of your body, and we've got to take every precaution to keep it stabilized."

"Oh, well," I said to him, "you can't have everything."

Then, just as all the sorrow had turned to joy, I got some bad news from Tina. She had received a phone call from Chicago telling her that her father had died; she'd be going back home for his funeral right away. "Darryl, Darryl," she said, crying, "what's happenin' to me? First it was you, and now it's my father. I don't know if I'm going to be able to handle all this. Everything's going against me and—"

I tried to console her, but it was no use.

"Tina," I said, "don't be angry. Your father lived a long and good life. God just took him home. You should be happy knowing that he's upstairs with Him. And you should be happy that I'm still here with you." Before I could finish, she was out the door and on her way home to Chicago for the funeral. I really felt for her.

A few days later, my mother, Wayne and Grannie Annie all returned to Chicago, and Tom Hoffman returned to Boston. Wayne had to teach high school classes, and he was already late for the fall semester. No sooner had they left than Tina returned, bringing with her some new pictures of the boys, plus some handwritten notes from them telling me to hurry on home to Chicago so they could see me.

Most of my days were filled from morning to night with therapy sessions, medical exams, and visitors. John Madden continued to stop by regularly, as did several of his Oakland players. Marvin Gaye, one of my favorite singers, was doing a gig in the Bay Area, and he came to see me two days in a row. "You'll always find strength in the Lord," said Marvin, who was deeply into religion.

"I always have and I hope I always will," I replied. "The Man already has given me a second life to lead for Him."

The only visitor I didn't like to see was my orderly friend, the guy in the green coat, the guy with the screwdriver who tightened the screws into my head. I was rough on him, but he took it well. "Buddy, lemme tell you one thing," I said to him one morning. "The day I finally start to walk again is the day I come back here to this hospital and screw some screws into your head twice a day, the way you've been doing to me. How do you think you'll like that?"

"I'd like it just about as much as you've liked it," he said. "Listen, Darryl, I don't want to hurt you. Honest, I don't. A long time ago I asked them if they'd have someone else do the work on you because I didn't want to hurt you anymore. But they didn't have anyone else to do it. Honest, I'll be as happy as you are the day they discharge you from this place." I felt awful.

"Well, hey, man, ahh, geez, I'm really sorry—"

"Forget it, Darryl," he said. "I knew that deep down you never meant any of the things you felt about me. I knew that once you got a chance to really think about me and about what I was doing for you, not to you, that you'd come around in your thinking."

"Yeah," I said. "And honest, I'm really sorry." He took my hand, held it tight for a second, and then left.

Except for my trips to the operating and diagnostic rooms, I didn't leave my little I.C. chamber for almost two months. And I spent most of my time—99.9 percent—on my Pancake. On two occasions the orderlies lifted me off the Pancake and tried to set me up in a chair, but they couldn't stabilize my head in a satisfactory position so abandoned the effort.

Being on the Pancake for so long, and being unable to move, I developed a number of deep bedsores. Three times a day a nurse would have to treat them and change the bandaging.

"We'd rather not put any bandages on these things," the nurse said to me, "but we have no choice in your case because you're lying on your back all the time and you'll just aggravate the sores if we don't cover them up." Boy, did they ever sting.

All the time I was in my chamber, my back was toward the only window in the room. I never got to see the light of day, or the lights of Castro Valley, which was the little town that Eden Hospital was in. I could look just one way, straight ahead, the direction depending upon the position of my Pancake.

Then, on September 18, several doctors and nurses and orderlies walked into my room at once. Good God, I thought, there's something wrong with me again. My lungs? Pneumonia? My neck? It's all over. What now? No, no, no . . . Then I saw Tina smiling, and all of a sudden everyone said, "Happy birthday, Darryl." That's right. I was now twenty-seven years old. And then they all sang "Happy Birthday" to me loud and clear.

I began to cry—God, I cried a lot in that hospital—and they rolled me out of my little room, into the main part of the I.C., and through a large door leading to the fire escape. There was a platform on the fire escape, and they flipped my Pancake into a position where I was looking directly into the sun. Was it ever spectacular. Light. The sun. Trees. People down there in the streets. Cars. Buildings. The whole world. A world I had not been a part of for so long.

We all had cake and ice cream out there on the fire escape, a real party. "Darryl," I thought, "all these people who are celebrating your twenty-seventh birthday today thought they'd be going to your funeral a few weeks ago." I couldn't stop crying.

Soon, too soon, the music stopped, the cake and the ice cream were gone, and I was back in my chamber, a prisoner again.

The next big dates on my calendar were September 22, 23, and 24, when the Patriots would be in Oakland to play the Raiders. From what Tina had been reading to me from the Boston newspapers, I knew this wasn't going to be any ordinary football game. The Patriots wanted to win the game for me, and they made no bones about it.

When you're confined to a small room and basically unable to move, you have a chance to do a lot of thinking, and once my bout with pneumonia ended in victory, I began to think a lot about Jack Tatum and what he did to me on the football field. It was clear to me and a lot of my New England teammates, that Tatum had taken an unnecessarily brutal shot at me. I had not caught the ball. I was no threat to him. Also, he'd come at me running full speed, and he'd had his bone—his forearm—cocked. I played football. I had played against some great defensive backs. Mel Blount of the Steelers had no equal, and he never took cheap shots at receivers, nor did Mike Haynes, against whom I worked every day in practice.

Jack Tatum could have pulled up. He could have stopped short of hitting me. And he certainly didn't have to nail me across the head and break my neck. But he had done it. I thought to myself,

"Darryl, Jack Tatum may have gotten you, but someday Jack Tatum's day will come."

The one thing I was certain of, though, was that none of my Patriot teammates would deliberately go out of their way to hit Tatum the way he had cheap-shotted me. The Patriots didn't play that way. And I, for one, always admired my team for that.

On Friday night, September 22, the Patriots arrived in Oakland for Sunday's game against the Raiders. First thing Saturday morning, Fairbanks came to visit and update me on the team. I already knew a lot of things about them. I had listened to the Patriots' first three games via a special radio set up in my room. My teammates, the Patriots organization, and Boston radio station WBZ paid the $500 to arrange a special phone line to my room, and I heard the games loud and clear. At some point during each game the announcers would stop their description of the play to say something like, "And now, let's say hello to someone who's listening to this game out near Oakland, California. Hello, Darryl, how are you? We're all rootin' and prayin' for you, Pal, and we'll all see you out there in a couple of weeks. Darryl Stingley, ladies and gentlemen, a man who has a lot of fight in him."

In fact, during the September 17 game between the Patriots and Baltimore, the WBZ radio engineer hooked his microphones to the public-address system at Schaefer Stadium at halftime, and I heard the announcer say to the crowd of more than 60,000 fans, "Ladies and gentlemen, and Patriot fans everywhere, tomorrow is the twenty-seventh birthday of a great New England Patriot... Number eighty-four, Darryl Stingley." The crowd's roar became terrific and almost drowned out the announcer's voice. "Ladies and gentlemen, Darryl's listening to this game in his hospital room out in California, so let's all sing 'Happy Birthday' to Darryl Stingley." And they did, all 60,000 of them, loud and clear.

Happy birthday to you,
Happy birthday to you,
Happy birthday dear Darryl.
Happy birthday to you.

There wasn't a dry eye in my room by the time the crowd finished that song. Not one.

"We should never have lost to Washington and Baltimore, Darryl," Fairbanks said, shaking his head. "We beat St. Louis, so we're one and two, but we should be three and zero. You know that. And we all know that we're going to beat the Raiders on Sunday night because we're playing this game for only one person: you. And that's enough to lift any team. Let's hope that beating the Raiders will give us the lift we need for the rest of the season. As I told you a few weeks back, the guys have been down ever since you got hurt."

I asked Chuck what time the team would be coming over.

"I thought about it a long time," he said, "and I think it's best that no one come until after the game. But as soon as that game's over, we'll be on our way here. You'd better be ready."

I watched the ABC telecast of the game and, needless to say, Howard Cosell kept telling the national audience that this was a very emotional game for the New England Patriots, that they were out to win the game for one of their fallen players—Number 84, Darryl Stingley, wide receiver from Purdue, who on this very field, on the night of August 12 last, was hit on the head by Jack Tatum, Number 32 of the Oakland Raiders, and suffered a broken neck and has been in Eden Hospital in nearby Castro Valley ever since, and probably will never walk again. . . . I thought that Howard and ABC overdid all the emotional and tear-jerking stuff, but that approach sells, I guess.

I knew we were going to win the game because I was refereeing. I called every play from my bed. Tina and I even had an argument when I said a Raider had clipped one of the Patriots. "That's no clip," she said as we watched the replay. "But look there, that Patriot sure is doing himself a whole lot of holding." She was right, too.

It was a close game, but we won, as I'd known we would, when Sam Cunningham scored a touchdown with just thirty-eight seconds to play. "Sam Bam," I said, "thank you, Man." I could hardly wait for him and Russ and all the guys to come walking into my room.

While my teammates were at the stadium changing into their street clothes, the nurses and doctors moved me out of the I.C. and took me to a large room down the corridor. "The last thing we want," said one of the nurses, "is for forty two-hundred-fifty-pound guys to come tromping through the doors of the I.C. making a lot of noise." CHIPS, the California Highway Patrol, gave the players a personal escort from the stadium to the hospital, violating California law in the process: no personal escorts by CHIPS, that's the law. But one of their officers had been paralyzed in a crash the week before, and they made a special provision in my case.

Suddenly, there they were . . . two dozen of my teammates, the ones who knew me best, the ones who could stand the sight of me, standing right alongside my bed. I'm sure they all wanted to crack a couple of jokes, but there wasn't a dry eye around.

"Here, Darryl, we brought you this," they said together. And they gave me the game ball, the same one Sam Cunningham had carried across the goal line for the winning touchdown. Then Raymond Berry, our receivers' coach, who had worked so hard with me in training camp, stepped forward and said, "Darryl, I've brought you this." He handed me a small silver frame with a quotation inside from Winston Churchill. The year before I had left one of those quotes in the locker of each of my teammates. I read the words, as I had so many times before:

Sure I am that this day we are masters of our fate; that the task which has been set before us is not above our strength; that its pangs and toils are not beyond our endurance. As long as we have faith in our own cause, and an unconquerable will to win, victory will not be denied us.

For some reason I had been scared to see my teammates. I accepted my situation, my condition, but I worried that what I represented to them was the worst thing they wanted to think about: a serious injury suffered during a football game. But when I actually saw them, for the first time since that night in August, I was excited, not scared. I wanted to prove to them that I could talk, so I talked a blue streak. I had a little joke for everyone, the private kind of joke that players have for players. I teased Al Chandler, the tight end, that he'd have to find some more speed if he ever wanted to fill in for me at wide receiver until I returned to the lineup. I kidded Sugar Bear Hamilton about his weight. I asked Russ Francis how his love life was going. I had the time of my life.

"Hey, guys," I said, "I'm probably not going to make it back for this season, but I'll be there in seventy-nine. This is only a temporary setback I've suffered." I really thought it was just that, a temporary setback.

They stayed with me for about an hour, or just about as long as my doctors allowed them. And then, one by one, they took my hand, said a few words of encouragement to me, and left the room to go to the airport for the charter flight back to New England.

"Geez," I thought, "this is the second charter flight in a row that I've missed from Oakland to New England." The orderlies wheeled me back into the I.C., and Tina and I cried ourselves to sleep.

Two weeks later, in early October, I finally got to make a chartered flight. It was late at night, and I don't remember much about it because I was heavily sedated.

"Darryl," Dr. Pont had said, "you're going home."

I was on my Pancake and Tina was at my side, as she always was those days. They rolled me out of the I.C., down a corridor, into an elevator and, finally, out some swinging doors directly into an ambulance. Then they drove me to the airport and wheeled me aboard a chartered medical jet. Doctor Birkenfeld and a nurse came aboard.

"Mind if we come along for the ride?" the nurse asked.

"Don't mind if you do," I said.

They gave me a sedative, and the last thing I remember is the plane taxiing down the runway to get into position for takeoff.

"When you wake up, Baby," Tina said, "we'll all be home in Chicago."

6 · Getting to Know the New Darryl

By 11:00 A.M., I was in my new home, the Rehabilitation Institute of Chicago. It was at the corner of Michigan and Superior in downtown Chicago, just a few blocks from the Near North Side, my old stomping grounds when the sun went down. They rolled my Pancake into a large ward and set it over in a corner, with a curtain surrounding me on three sides. There was so much screaming and hollering and crying going on in the ward that I couldn't think.

"You won't be here for long," a nurse said. "A private room will be opening on the sixth floor in just a few days, and it's been reserved for you. Just have some patience and bear with us, would you, please?"

My second or third day in that ward—I had lost all real track of time—I overheard a male voice, a doctor's voice, I guessed, telling someone, "And this is one of our wards for quads." It sounded so poetic: wards for quads. Suddenly, it hit me. "If this is a ward for quads, and I'm in this ward for quads, then I must be one of those quads."

But what was a quad? That night I asked one of the nurses what a quad was.

"A quadriplegic," she said, sounding rather gloomy.

"Am I one of these quadriplegics?" I asked her, stumbling over the word quadriplegic.

"It looks that way, I'm afraid, Darryl," she said.

"Well, what is this quadriplegic thing anyway?" I asked her.

"Quads, Darryl," she said, "are people who are unable to function from neck to toes. At this point you cannot function from your neck to your toes. That might change in time, of course, but for now you have been classified as a quadriplegic." A quadriplegic! I didn't even know how to spell the word. I knew of people who had been paralyzed after being in an accident, but I had never heard of anyone who was a quadriplegic.

It took a while—weeks, really—for what that nurse told me to sink in. I never wanted to discuss this new condition of mine with anyone. Not Tina. Not my mother. Not my father. Not the doctors. Not the nurses. No one. It was my affliction, my new state in life, and I'd handle it my own way, deal with it on my own terms.

I immediately became depressed. Totally depressed. Suddenly I was not sure of anything. Where am I going? What am I going to do? Who am I? What am I? What about my sex life? What about Tina and my boys? Who would provide for them the rest of their lives? How was I going to be able to do any of the things that I once used to do so naturally? Will I ever take another step? Everything from A to Z.

It was a real shocker to hear first-hand that the doctors didn't think I'd ever walk again. And all the time I'd been imagining getting back into my Patriots uniform, trotting onto the field to a tremendous standing ovation—and then catching a couple of touchdown passes to lead my team to victory.

I had tremendous confidence in my natural physical ability; I

always thought I could overcome any physical limitation or problem. I thought the injury I had suffered on the football field in
Oakland was just a minor setback. I had thought my physical
ability would let me bust out of the Pancake, out of the infernal
halo, and crash back onto the football field—triumphant once
more. Yes, I thought, someday it would all be so beautiful once
again.

But now I had been told that I'd probably never take another
step. Barring a miracle, I had played my last football game.
Barring a miracle, I would never walk again. A miracle. . . .

"Darryl," I said to myself, "God doesn't give any one man very
many miracles. You probably used up your share when you survived the pneumonia and the collapsed lung, the night everyone
expected you to die. It's probably too much to expect that He'll be
performing any more miracles for you."

I immediately made a promise to myself: I'd make them pay.
"Them" was everyone. I decided right away that I'd treat the
Rehab Institute as a foreign and hostile place. I would do everything in my power to let the doctors, nurses and therapists know
that I hated it there and I'd make life absolutely miserable for
everyone who came into contact with me. The way I saw it, no
matter what you call it, an institution is a place where foreign
forces try to gain control of your mind. Ain't no way they were
going to control my mind. No way. I'd show them. I'd beat them
away.

After about a week in the ward for quads, I finally got some
peace and quiet. My private room was ready, and I had private-
duty nurses twenty-four hours a day. Just as I was settling into my
new home, a lady in a white coat walked through the door and said
in a cheerful voice, "Lunch, Mr. Stingley."

"Get out of here and take that junk with you," I snapped. "I'm
not eating that crap. And I'll eat when I want to eat. Aren't you
supposed to bring me a menu and let me order what I want? I

137

wouldn't eat that stuff if you paid me." The lady was taken aback, and she ran out of the room. "That'll teach them," I thought. But no one ever came back and brought me lunch.

A couple of days later there was a knock on my door.

"Hello?" I said.

"Mr. Stingley, may I come in?"

"Sure," I said. Then this guy opened the door and walked into the room. He announced that he was the staff psychiatrist.

"Get the hell out of here, Man," I yelled at him when I heard who he was. "I don't need no shrink. I don't need your bullshit." No way I was talking to any psychiatrist. What did I need help for? "I'll be my own shrink," I told the psychiatrist. "No way I'm going to let you sit around here and pick my brain and ask me a lot of questions. You don't know me. You don't know what it's like to lie here every day."

"That's why I'm here," the psychiatrist said. "I want to find out about you, about who you are."

"I know who I am," I said. "Let me ask you the questions. You just want to ask me a lot of stupid and silly questions so you can categorize me as being one thing or another, don't you?"

"Mr. Stingley, I've got to come and see you anyway," the psychiatrist said, "and I'm going to get paid for it whether you talk to me or not."

"I don't care what you do with the time you spend with me," I said, "but I have nothing, not a damned thing, to talk to you about." And we never talked, not once, during my six months at the Rehab. I wasn't taking any mental trips with any shrink.

Late one night, one of my nurses thought she'd try a different game plan with me. "Darryl," she said when she came in to put out my lights, "you're getting to be known around here as the worst patient we have. It's your attitude. You've got a bad attitude, the worst a lot of us have ever come across." I wasn't ready for that.

"Listen," I said to her. "My attitude is bad, I know that. But I think you people should have expected my attitude to be what it's been. I think you people should be trained to cope with the negative attitudes of the people undergoing all this rehabilitation. You people expect me to accept the rehabilitation programs you've made up with no questions asked. That's not easy for me to do, certainly not right away."

"Darryl," she said, "I understand where you're coming from. But just give us a break, and give yourself a break. Things take time, and you're not giving us—or yourself—the time to make it work."

I thought about what she said after she turned off the lights and left the room. I wasn't having out-and-out fights with the people at the Rehab. Or at least I didn't think I was fighting with them. The way I saw it, I was what you'd call standoffish. About everything. I remembered the old Darryl. Darryl the physical being. With the old Darryl, the physical side always dominated the mental side. I was a physical stud, a horse. All a horse does is run, and that's all Darryl Stingley the physical being ever did. I was always moving. I was playing basketball, football, baseball. I was dancing and jiving. I was the ultimate active individual. I was always thinking about having a good time, and then I was having that good time. I tried to be well balanced, to be a little of everything, but in the end I was a creature of the physical, a creature of action. There was no getting around that.

Now, suddenly, here in the Rehab, I had to face up to life, to do things that didn't come easily or naturally. And up to now I always had an outlet—an excuse, I now realized—to run away from anything I didn't want to deal with directly. A lab class at Purdue? Sorry, I have football practice. Problems with Tina? Sorry, I got to get back to Boston for training camp. Here, for the first time in my life, I had no escape. That, as I saw it, was my problem, and I'd have to find the answer. But, for the moment, it was more than I could handle.

The real problem, though I didn't realize it at the time, was that the old Darryl was no more. The new Darryl—Darryl the quad—had to get to know himself, to understand what made him tick.

My understanding with the Rehab Institute was that it wouldn't make any public announcements that I was being treated there. I didn't want distractions. The only people who knew where I was were the members of my immediate family, the Patriots, and my agent in Boston, Jack Sands. My name had pretty much dropped from the newspapers after it had been reported I had beaten death and survived pneumonia and a collapsed lung back in California. People had forgotten about me. And I liked it that way. I didn't need any distractions. Not just yet.

I thought that everything was in place on this front, until one night, watching the sports on TV, I heard Tim Weigel, one of the local commentators, say something like, "Darryl Stingley, the fallen Patriot, is back in town at the Rehabilitation Institute over on Superior." How the hell did he find out that I was in Chicago?

Within moments my phone was ringing off the wall. I knew a few of the callers, but most were strangers. Those I knew all wanted to come see me. Like right now.

"Hey, Darryl, how're ya doing?"

"Darryl, this is me, Ron. We went to school together at Marshall High, remember?"

"Darryl, you don't know me, but I just want you to know that we've been prayin' for your recovery ever since your accident."

"Ah, I'm sorry," I told everyone, "but the doctors won't let anyone in to see me for a few more months." I didn't want to see those people, so I lied.

Once the rest of the Chicago press heard that I was in town, the public relations office at the Rehab Institute was swamped with calls asking if I'd give interviews.

"Listen," I finally shouted at one of those P.R. people. "My wishes aren't very complicated. I just want to be left alone, all the time. I don't want people bugging me with their cameras and their tape recorders. I'm not ready for that, don't you understand? Now get out of here!"

But the requests continued, and after several days one of my doctors said to me, "Darryl, it's really about time that you faced the press and made a statement."

My reaction to that was quick and sharp. "Whaddya mean it's about time I faced the press?" I said. "I'll face the press when I want to—and only when I want to. That's the way it's gonna happen, do you hear?"

The press, though, wouldn't take no for an answer. Guys would call me all the time, asking me for an exclusive interview. "Darryl, this is so and so of the so and so," they would start . . . but before they could get the next words out of their mouths, they'd get an earful.

One morning a lady from the P.R. office came to my room and said, "Darryl, we know you don't want to talk to the press, but a reporter from the *Chicago Sun-Times* is down in the lobby and he says he's going to camp out there until he gets to talk to you. Why don't you be a nice guy and talk to him?"

"I hope he's got a lot of water in his canteen," I said to the P.R. lady, "'cause he'll have to camp out there for a couple of months, until I'm ready to see him."

"Darryl, the writer's name is Ron Rappaport, and he seems like such a nice man."

"He probably is, but I'm not a nice person right now, and I don't want to talk to anyone—not anyone—while I'm feeling like this."

"But Darryl," she said, "they've got to take you right through the lobby at noontime on your way to physical therapy, and seeing this Mr. Rappaport wouldn't be any trouble at all."

"Move him out of there, or else I'm not going to physical therapy."

"But Darryl, we just can't tell him to leave." For all I know, Ron Rappaport is still camped out in the lobby, waiting for me to come through. I didn't go to my physical-therapy session that day.

Another day I was taking a nap in my room, and when I woke up there were a dozen people standing around my bed looking me over. One of my doctors was conducting a tour of the Rehab's facilities and, as he put it, "I brought these people here to see one of our star patients." Star patient my ass.

"Get out of here right now, all of you," I shouted loud and clear. "I'm not a star patient. And I'm not on exhibit for anyone."

My bitchiness seemed to have no bounds. One nurse said to me, "Darryl, you're one tough cookie. If you die while you're in here, you're going to go straight to hell. Nonstop. You're giving everyone here a whole lot more trouble than you're worth."

I didn't know if she was a hundred percent right about that. I just knew I wasn't ready to face society. Not yet. Nothing was clearly fixed in my mind. My thoughts changed by the minute. What I felt about someone, or something, changed 180 degrees by the next moment. I still hadn't formulated any solid opinions on what had happened to me, or why it had happened to me, and I didn't want to be running off at the mouth until I had everything in clear focus. Was that too much to ask?

That period when I was "getting to know Darryl," as I put it, was the toughest part of my stay at the Rehab. Athletics had always been the main part of my life, and I had a great deal of pride in my ability as an athlete. I could do everything in athletics. Everything. It was my whole identity. People knew me not as Darryl Stingley but as Darryl Stingley, athlete. Now I had to come to grips with the fact that it would never be the same again. As a result, Darryl the athlete and Darryl the quad were in constant conflict. It was a war. I'd be up, I'd be down. I'd be down, I'd be up. I'd never be in between.

During those first few months I was at my worst in the daily physical-therapy class. The physical therapists made no bones about the fact that their motto was: No pain, no gain. Unfortunately, I wasn't much for more pain at the time, being in enough pain—mental and physical—as it was, and when the therapists would physically grab me and bend me and shape me to see how much movement I had, how flexible I was, how much weight I could bear on my limbs, well, the pain became unbearable. It sure was one helluva lot more painful than getting hit by some big tackle on a football field.

I was working with a particular therapist, a woman, and she tried to get me to do some strenuous excercises that I hadn't tried before.

"No way I can do what you want me to do," I said to her. "I can't handle it."

"Do it, and do it now," she said sharply.

I think that she thought, "Hey, this guy's an old football player. A pro in the NFL. He's used to the tough stuff. I'm going to let it all hang out with him." So she tried to find out what I was made of. It was part of her little psychological game: She simply wanted me to do something that I didn't feel I was capable of doing. So she put me onto a heavily padded mat on the floor, then rolled me onto my stomach. After that she set my elbows underneath me, in what she called the triangular shape.

"Now what I want you to do isn't complicated at all," she said. "I just want you to hold yourself up for as long as you can. Brace yourself up."

God, in the old days—those before August 12, 1978—I could do dozens of push-ups with my fingertips.

"I can't do it," I cried, as my elbows collapsed under the weight. "The pain is too much."

I couldn't brace my weak 140-pound body on my elbows, that's how bad things were for me. I also had developed what was later to be diagnosed as tendinitis in both shoulders, and they were very tender to the touch. When I was up on my elbows the way she wanted me to be, the pain in my shoulders was worse than hell. I cried some more.

"Is it always going to be like this?" I asked the therapist. "Is this the way you people are going to treat me? Will it always be so painful?"

I expected some sympathy from her, but what I got was "Darryl, you make me sick when you cry."

I was shattered. I cried some more. And some more. I was filled with rage.

"I'll show you, you bitch," I said to her. I wanted to lash out and swing at her, curse her, but I managed to control myself. Anyway, I couldn't swing at her. Still, the pain was more than I could handle. No sooner was I back in my room than there was a knock on the door,

"Darryl, it's Dr. Vinod Sahgal. May I come in?"

I couldn't tell Dr. Sahgal, the assistant director of the Rehab Institute, that he couldn't come into my room. He came over to my bed and made small talk for a minute.

"Now, Doc, I know you're not here just to ask me how I like things," I said.

"You're right, Darryl. I'll be up front with you. A lot of people are coming to me and complaining about your attitude and the way you do your work. They say you're the worst patient they've ever encountered. I want you to know that I listen to them. But I also want you to know that I've told them to do their work and not worry about your attitude, that you'll figure that out for yourself. I like your attitude, myself. You're a fighter, Darryl, and I like that. The problem around here is that not too many of the patients are fighters. Most of them have just about given up and accepted their conditions. You're trying to beat yours, and I understand that. I like it.

"But Darryl, between you and me, I think you really ought to change your attitude. You've got nothing to gain if you keep on treating everyone the way you have since you arrived. You may not think so, but they're trying to help you. So, my advice to you, Darryl, is to get smart. Don't fight the therapists. Work hand in hand with them. You and everyone else will be a lot better off in the end." And then he left the room.

I thought about what he said, about his advice, and I made a conscious decision. From now on Darryl Stingley would look out for Darryl Stingley and no one else. But while Darryl was looking out for Darryl, he'd be considerate of the people he was dealing with on a regular basis.

I told Tina what Doctor Sahgal had said when she visited later that day, and she gave me one of her I-told-you-so answers. She'd been on my case, too, trying to get me to calm down, to show some respect for the people trying to help me get rid of my bad attitude. "I'm not gonna say another word about it," she said. "But if you weren't so darn stubborn and had listened to me the last few days, I could have saved you from having Doctor Sahgal come in here. But it's over and done with, so now let's forget it."

The trick, as I saw it, would be to eliminate the negative from my mind—the bitterness, the frustration, the depressing thoughts. The more negative I was, the more likely I was to be on the destructive side. And if I self-destructed to any serious degree, particularly in a place like the Rehab Institute, I'd weaken myself to the point where I'd probably just want to give up.

It was all there in black and white, and I had learned all there was about black and white when I was a kid. It was either/or in the streets; either *them* or *you*. You were part of a gang and headed for reform school or prison or the graveyard—or you weren't part of a gang. You didn't make it—or you made it. A lot of the kids I grew up with didn't make it, because they succumbed to crime or to drugs, and now they're either six feet under or serving time or living their day-to-day lives in the same old streets with no purpose whatsoever. I was a survivor of the streets of Chicago. And I'd be a survivor of this Rehab Institute.

My new strategy was to roll with the punches. I'd fight, sure I'd fight, but I wouldn't do it negatively. Everything would be positive from now on. I'd think 100 percent positive all the way. The next day when I went to physical therapy, the same therapist was on duty, and she put me through the same torture tests as the day before. I thought to myself, "This lady is still one tactless bitch," but I kept my mouth shut for a change—and did what I was told.

I also began to think about why she was tormenting me so, and when I came up with my own answers, I began to gain some respect for her. I decided that she was treating me differently from the other patients, that she was more demanding of me because she didn't think I'd be demanding enough of myself. "Darryl," I said, "she's just playing a little mind game with you. If she wins, you win. If you win, she wins. Whatever happens, Darryl, you win the game." I could see that with her negative attitude and approach, the therapist was trying to motivate me indirectly. She was challenging me. And in my desire to prove to her that she couldn't beat me down with her mind games, I advanced to the point where there was nothing I wouldn't try. Maybe I'd be able to do it, maybe I wouldn't, but I always tried.

"Let's do that brace up exercise you put me in yesterday," I said to her.

"Why?" she said, shaking her head. "You couldn't do it yesterday. You said it was too tough for you."

"That was yesterday," I said. "Lemme try it again right now."

"You sure?" she said.

"Yeah, I'm sure."

She rolled me over on the mat and set me up in the triangle shape, the way she had the day before.

"All right," she said, "I'm gonna let go, and then I'll start counting. Let's see if you can make it to five."

She let go. I felt as though I was holding up the John Hancock Building—all 103 stories.

"One Mississippi, two Mississippi, three Mississippi, four—" I couldn't bear the pain any longer, and my elbows gave out.

"Darryl, that's fantastic," the therapist said. "You braced yourself for almost four whole seconds."

Four whole seconds! It sounded like a world's indoor record. "And the winner of the elbow brace-up, in a world's record of three and one half seconds, Number Eighty-four, Darryl Stingley." Well, it was a beginning anyway.

Back in my room that night I fully reconciled myself to my quadriplegia, and vowed to beat it. Only my definition of "beat," in this case, was "accept." Really accept it. Over the previous twenty-four hours, and, indeed, over the previous two or three months, I had discovered that I was a lot tougher and had a lot more intestinal fortitude than I thought I had. I knew I wasn't a quitter. That had been put to the test and I had come out victorious. I could have quit, just like that, any day. I could have quit on life. I learned later that six of ten quadriplegics attempt suicide at least once, but that thought never entered my mind. I never once thought of taking away the life that God had twice given me. Quadriplegia or not, there was too much to live for.

The way I figured it, my time had come early. Every football player reaches that day when his career comes to an end and he is faced with the question: What do I do now? I had put a lot of time, all my time, into developing my body to play games, and as a result, most of my confidence was based on my athletic ability. "Darryl," I said, "the best way to look at it is that you've just taken early retirement as a football player and begun your new career."

As for what that new career would be, I didn't know the answer yet. But I was a celebrity of sorts—the football player who had been struck down by a vicious hit during a game and now was a quadriplegic—and I'd definitely take advantage of that. When I got out of the Rehab Institute, I'd be active in my community. I'd try to be a humanitarian. With my condition, with the opportunities that would be available to me because of my celebrity, it would be silly not to take the lead in various ways.

"Darryl, everybody's looking for a hero," I told myself that night. "Everybody's looking for someone to cling to. That can be you. That *should* be you. You can be someone for kids, parents, grandparents—everyone—to look up to, to admire. And if you do it right, Darryl, people will look at you and say, 'Hey, he was a football player, and he had an injury, but that didn't stop him. Look, he's really helping people.' " I told myself, "Darryl, don't blow this opportunity that God has given you to do for others what He has done for you." And you know what? I slept better that night than I had in months.

With everything now firmly settled in my mind, I was able to go about my rehabilitation with a clear head, and that made things better for everyone. My days became a mix of therapy, inspection, private thought, and family visits. In many ways the seven months I spent at the Rehab Institute were like a silent movie. I stared at things and at people all day. I saw people curled up, all bent over. I was in bad enough shape, but they were in tougher shape. Compared to some of the patients, I had it good.

Each day I was awake by 7:00 A.M. I certainly didn't like getting up that early, but I didn't have much choice. Everyone else on the sixth floor was awake, and the halls were bustling with nurses and doctors. It was really raw in the winter because my room was on a corner, and the cold winds blowing off Lake Michigan, just a block or two away, seemed to blast through the walls of the Institute. "You know," I complained to a nurse one frosty morning, "I'll bet they never put any insulation in these walls. If I didn't have all these blankets on me every night, I'd freeze to death."

My nurse would bathe me, and then I'd have breakfast. At mealtime I always ate as much as I could. My weight was down below 150 pounds, and I thought I looked like a scarecrow. "Darryl," I said, "Mean Joe Greene and all those dudes'd bend you up like a pretzel, spit you out, and step all over you, the way you are now." But no matter how much I ate, I wasn't able to put on many pounds.

Physical therapy was next, at 10:00 A.M. sharp. The therapists would work with me on breathing, teaching me how to get maximum output from my lungs, which had been under such strain during my stay in the hospital in California, and working to develop muscle tone by taking me through an involved series of voluntary and involuntary movements.

After that I'd go back to my room for lunch and a nap. In the afternoon I had two more therapy sessions—first an occupational therapy class, where the therapists would work with me individually to create ways for me to adjust to my new environment, and then another exercise-type therapy program, where they'd bend and twist my arms, my body, and my legs to improve my blood circulation, followed by a dip in the therapy pool. Following that painful exercise I'd go back to my room, have an early dinner, see visitors, watch TV, talk on the phone—and fall asleep.

Boring? Yes. But a lot less boring than being in a box six feet down.

Tina was a Rock of Gibraltar during my stay at the Rehab, just as she had been in California. She came by every day for an hour and did what she could to help the nurses and therapists. If she timed her visit with the arrival of one of my meals, she'd take over the feeding chores from the nurse. "All right, open wide," she'd say, and I'd open as wide as I could, which wasn't very wide, and she'd slip the food into my mouth.

My mother didn't visit me too often, once a week at most, but she phoned about every other day. She wanted to visit every day, I knew, but she wasn't up to it. She had had a tough time handling her visits at the hospital in California, and she still got all wound up and emotional and hypertense when she saw me in the Rehab.

"Don't worry, Mom," I said to her, "I'm all right now, so there's no reason to get yourself worked up, which is what'll happen if you visit every day."

My father, who had remarried and was living on Chicago's South Side, visited every Monday and Thursday night like clockwork. He'd finish work, jump into his car, and then he'd be at my door. He missed only one Monday night in seven months, and that was when the city of Chicago was totally shut down because of a snowstorm. "Sorry, Darryl, but I can't even get out the door, the snow's piled so high," he said on the phone, apologizing for his absence.

"I can't get out the door because they won't let me," I said. And we both laughed.

On the nights my father'd come to see me, he had a funny way of announcing himself. Like a lot of people, my father thought that someday I might make a sudden reflexive movement that would, in a sense, shock me out of my paralysis. So he'd come to my door, look in—and then throw a wad of Kleenex or toilet paper at my bed.

"Hi, Dad," I'd say when I'd see the missile coming at me. "I've got bad hands today. I can't catch anything."

My father and I never talked about serious stuff, just how I was coping and what was happening in the sports world.

"Your Patriots sure got their act together," he said to me one night toward the end of November.

"Yep," I said, "since that night they beat the Raiders in Oakland and gave me the game ball, they've won nine of ten games. Chuck Fairbanks thought that seeing me would give 'em a lift, and I guess it did. Nine of ten. Hey, they've got themselves a chance to go all the way and win the Super Bowl. If they do, you can bet I'll get to that game."

Aside from Tina, the person I saw most was my Uncle Ed—Ed Brown, my mother's brother. He had long been a solid friend and he was always around the hospital trying to help me out and do little things for me. He was my right-hand man. There were a lot of things I didn't like to ask the nurses to do for me—you can probably imagine what they were—so I'd just ask Uncle Ed to do them, and he would see to them right away.

"Me and you'd make a good team, Darryl," Uncle Ed said one day.

"Not in sports, Uncle Ed," I kidded him, "you're not too good going to your left."

For the first five or six weeks I was in the Rehab I also got regular twice-a-day visits from an orderly (he wore white, not green) who'd screw the halo I still had to wear tighter into my scalp. I didn't bleed as much as I had in California, but there was always some blood on my face when he got finished. I took a new tack with the orderlies at the Rehab, too: I ignored them. I figured the less I saw of them, the better for all concerned, so when they'd come in, I'd zip my lips until they left. That was before I made my peace with the new Darryl.

"What's the matter, Mr. Stingley, don't you have anything to say?" one of the orderlies said to me just after I arrived.

"Yep, I have just one thing to say to you," I said. "Do your work and get out of here as fast as you can. And don't let the door hit you on your way out." He got my drift.

Then, just before Thanksgiving, about six weeks into my stay, a couple of orderlies and a doctor and a nurse walked into my room unannounced.

"Good news today, Mr. Stingley," the doctor said. "The halo's coming off." Hallelujah! One of the orderlies took his screwdriver and, instead of twisting the screws deeper into my scalp, unscrewed them. The other orderly disconnected the apparatus that hitched the eighty-pound weight to the halo. The doctor then bandaged the area where the screws had been implanted into my scalp.

"No more crown of thorns," I said happily. "And now I'll be able to look at myself in the mirror."

But best of all, I'd be able to see my boys. Just about every day Tina had begged me to let the boys come to the Rehab with her, but I'd always told her no. I couldn't stand the thought of having them see me with the halo around my head. That was not the father they knew. To me, being in bed, unable to move a muscle, was one thing, but being in bed, unable to move a muscle, with a halo around my head was the worst of all possible things. Now, at last, they wouldn't be scared when they saw me.

I asked the nurse to call Tina at the apartment, where she was living with Hank, Derek, and my mother, and tell her that when she came to see me, she should bring the boys with her. The nurse dialed the number, gave Tina the message and ended by saying, " . . . and he'd really like you to drop everything and get here as fast as you can."

I took a nap and was dozing when Hank and Derek finally walked through the door for the first time. I didn't know what to say to them. Hank came over first and held my hand and then kissed me. Derek did the same thing. And then we all started to cry—Hank, Derek, Tina, and me. I couldn't stop.

"I love you guys," I said to them. "I'm really proud of both of you. I'll always love you and be proud of you. Always." I had to stop talking for a minute while Tina wiped the tears from my face.

"Ahh, listen, guys," I said, "I'd sure love to jump out of this bed and go outside to throw a football around, but it doesn't look like I'll be able to play any more ball again. But I'm gonna come home for good someday soon, and we'll all be together and I'll be with you every step of the way."

I had a million questions to ask them, and they had all the answers.

"Yes, Dad, we're doing our schoolwork."

"No, Dad, we're not hangin' around with the wrong guys."

"Yes, Dad, we're helping Mom around the apartment."

I didn't want them to leave, but after a while they had to go—and a little bit of me went out the door with them. Oh, how I was looking forward to going home myself. The subject of marriage had not come up in my conversations with Tina, but it was very much on my mind—if she wanted it. She was happy, as well

152

as I could tell. The boys both looked great, strong and healthy, and sharp as tacks. The only thing missing from the picture was me.

Once that infernal halo was taken off my head for good, I was introduced to a whole new world: that of the wheelchair.

"Darryl," a nurse joked, "now you're gonna be a big wheel."

That first wheelchair I had was your basic standard issue, nothing more, and I had to be pushed around by an attendant or by my nurse. I didn't like that, either, because I wanted to stop and chat with people I met. You see a pretty face, you want to say hello. Right? Well, I did. Unfortunately, the nurses and attendants had better things to do with their time.

Then one day the therapists suggested I try what they called a sip-and-puff chair. It looked like any other wheelchair, but it had a straw that came up to mouth level. You were supposed to operate the chair with sips and puffs of air. You'd puff through the straw to make the chair go forward, sip air in to make the chair go backward, and blow some other crazy way if you wanted to make it turn.

That sip-and-puff chair was just one fine example of the wonderful things those therapists at the Rehab were doing to help people like me. It took me a while to give them the great credit they deserved, to stop fighting them, something I sincerely regret now. Those people are geniuses. They spend every day of their lives trying to invent things to help disabled people to be more independent. I should have appreciated that sooner.

But let's face it. There's no more helpless feeling in the world than asking someone to push you over here, over there, everywhere. Even so, I wasn't very receptive to the sip-and-puff chair. Using it seemed like one helluva lot of work, and when you came right down to it, I didn't know what I was doing. But in keeping with my new motto—"Try everything"—I gave it a whirl.

God, I looked like Darryl Stingley, Number 84, ace driver in the demolition derby on "Wide World of Sports." I drove that

153

chair into walls, crashed into people, and almost careened down a flight of stairs.

"That's it for me," I announced. "No more of this sippin' and puffin'. I'll kill myself at this rate." Fact was, I couldn't see myself sippin' and puffin' my way around town for the rest of my life, even if a wheelchair was going to be my main means of transportation. So it was back to the old-fangled wheelchair, with someone pushing me everywhere.

Then one day a therapist in my exercise class noticed that I had the slightest bit of movement in my right hand and arm. Not much, but some. Maybe a millimeter. Maybe two. Whatever, there was movement. He checked out my left arm completely, but there was no motion or movement there whatsoever. So the physical therapists immediately began to concentrate on exercising my right arm and hand and developing whatever movement had been detected. Meanwhile, the physical therapists had informed the occupational therapists—the Rehab was running over with therapists of all sorts—of that movement in my right arm. They all concluded that I had just enough dexterity with my right arm and hand to operate a wheelchair—if, that is, they could find a way to get my hand on the control. And so they went to work inventing a button that would permit me to control a chair. By myself.

"Darryl, have we got a surprise for you today," a therapist told me several days later. "You're going to take a trip all by yourself."

"Where to?" I said. "Hong Kong?" Even when I was on my better behavior, sometimes I didn't make things any easier for myself. That was not the time for jokes.

"Darryl, you can go anywhere you want to," the therapist said. "Just don't get lost." And then they lifted me out of my bed and plunked me down into the jazziest wheelchair I'd ever seen.

"What's this?" I asked them.

"A Medi-Cline chair," one of the therapists said.

"This has got to be the Cadillac of wheelchairs," I said.

"No, it's the *Q.E. II* of wheelchairs," one of the therapists said, laughing.

"It sure is."

It was like something from another planet. The chair had buttons and gadgets everywhere. It was fully powered by a big battery, stashed underneath the seat. The seat itself could slide forward or backward. And if you dropped the seat into a horizontal position, the footrest would automatically rise up to make, well, the foot of a bed.

"Darryl," one of the therapists said, "you can work this chair yourself just by playing with this button right here." The button was more of a switch, set at the end of the little platform that formed the armrest for my right arm and hand. "See this?" the therapist said, and then he moved the button forward. My chair lurched forward about five feet.

"What are you guys trying to do, kill me?"

Well, after giving me all sorts of instructions, they wheeled me out into the lounge area on the sixth floor and left me there all alone. "We'll see you in about an hour," they said, and then they just walked away and disappeared.

As I sat there in this gadget-packed Cadillac, I was having normal reactions for a quad—hot flashes, cold flashes, dizzy spells. I had been blacking out every so often during my physical-therapy sessions, and now I was afraid that I'd black out again.

I fought to keep my head up, a job in itself. And I looked straight down the corridor to my room at the other end. It was probably a distance of, oh, twenty-five yards, but it looked like twenty-five miles to me. I thought of my room as a paradise and I had to get there. If I could, I could get into my bed again and relax. I could take a nap. I could get a few calls put through. I could do anything I wanted.

So what did I do? I sat in my wheelchair in the lounge and cried like a baby. I was scared. But not for long. "Why cry, Darryl, why cry?" I said to myself over and over. "Don't cry. Now's the time to kick ass. Suck it up, Darryl, and get moving."

I tried to put my predicament in a football perspective. I had just caught a pass at the 25-yard line and had to get into that end zone. Trouble was, there were eleven guys in front of me who didn't want me to make it. What to do?

Slowly, painfully, oh so painfully, I worked the index finger of my right hand against the control switch on the armrest, and the chair started to move forward. I pulled my right hand back off the button—actually it was a slow and painful retraction—and the Medi-Cline stopped. Then I slowly worked the switch back toward me, and the chair began to move in reverse. I experimented with that switch for what seemed like an eternity. If I maneuvered the button to the left, the chair went left; if I worked it to the right, the chair went right. God, I had a new toy, and I was like a little kid. It was all so simple, yet so painful, too.

Suddenly that end zone—my room—was no obstacle at all. It took me more than an hour to cover the twenty-five yards from the foyer to my room. The chair bolted forward, weaved to the right, jumped into reverse, made a U-turn, slammed into a wall, lurched to the left—but I kept making progress, shortening that distance to my haven in Room 604. Finally, I was there, in the end zone, and as I turned the chair ever so slowly to steer it into my room, I heard a lot of commotion behind me. I couldn't see what was happening, so I maneuvered the chair back and forth until I was able to look back down the corridor.

What a sight! Standing there in the middle of the corridor, about halfway between my room and the lounge, was a whole bunch of doctors, nurses, and therapists, and they were clapping. For me! I was getting a standing ovation. My first standing ovation since I was taken off that field in Oakland on a stretcher, and I hadn't been able to hear anything that night.

"Darryl, you made it, you made it," they all shouted.

"Yep, I made it," I said. And to paraphrase Neil Armstrong

when he became the first man to walk on the moon, "One little wheelchair trip down the corridor for Darryl Stingley, one giant step forward for Darryl Stingley."

For weeks the people at the Rehab had been preaching independence to me, and I hadn't been buying it. My solo ride down the corridor became Step Number One. After that, nobody at the Rehab ever pushed me around in a wheelchair. I drove myself everywhere. And I became a champ with that chair. It became a part of me, a part of my life. In many ways, it is me. I'd like to think that I could make my chair fly if I had to.

My favorite therapy classes, though, were with the people in the occupational session. I worked very closely with Judy Ranka, and we hit if off right away, probably because she didn't try to play any mind games with me. She was up front and direct all the time, not looking for an edge.

Basically, the occupational therapists examined me to see what movement I had, or didn't have, and then tried to create environments in which I could function. For instance, during one of our conversations they discovered I was deep into music, so they created a special tape recorder that I could activate simply by pushing one little switch, the same way I worked the switch that controlled my wheelchair.

For several weeks Judy and her friends worked to develop an intricate brace system that would allow me to use a pen or pencil and do some writing. They'd come to me with a unit, assemble it on me, then shake their heads and take it off. A few days later they'd be back with another unit for me to try.

"You people sure like playin' with your erector sets," I kidded one of them.

"Be patient, Darryl," he said. "We're going to find the right brace for you yet."

And they did. My right arm and my right hand were able to be braced in such a way that I could handle a pencil and write. Of course, the first few times I tried the new brace, it took an hour for

157

me to write the first two letters of my name—D . . . A . . .—but within a couple of months I was able to write my whole name for the first time—D . . . A . . . R . . . R . . . Y . . . L—and not take all day to do it. Judy was absolutely ecstatic, almost as much as I was, and we just about had a party.

Next, Judy wanted me to learn how to type. She was one of those really speedy typists herself; she could make the keyboard sing.

"Judy," I said to her, "forget it. I don't know where the Q is or the V or the L. I've never used a typewriter in my life. Whenever I wanted a paper typed at Purdue, I'd get some girl in the athletic office to do it for me."

"That's all right, Darryl," she said, "but let's just give it a try anyway."

So we did.

She put a typewriter on a counter across the front of my chair, and using my right hand—the only one I could move—I started to hunt and peck away and print out my thought for the day. It'd take me an hour to type a little three or four word sentence, but I always got a tremendous feeling of fulfillment and achievement when I saw my words on paper.

One day I asked one of my nurses, Barbara Bradford, what the occupational therapists did with my typing and writing papers. "They throw that stuff away as junk?" I asked.

"Probably," she said. "Who'd want 'em?"

She knew what I was thinking, though, and while I was sleeping that afternoon, Barbara went to see the occupational therapists, confiscated my old papers, brought them back to my room, and put them on the bulletin board over my head.

When I woke up Barbara said, "Surprise!"—and pointed to my brilliant efforts.

"The works of Darryl," I said, sounding mock-serious.

"Yes," she said, "the works of Darryl." I'm sure that what she'd rather have said was "Darryl's a piece of work."

By Christmastime the doctors at the Rehab were so impressed with my improvement and my overall condition, and my gradual change in attitude, that they decided I deserved a treat.

"Darryl," said one doctor, "we're going to let you go home for a few days to stay with your family."

Go home? Me go home? I couldn't wait to tell Tina the good news when she came to see me that night.

"I've got a Christmas present for you," I said.

"What is it?" she said.

"Me."

And so one morning they put me in my Medi-Cline chair, strapped me up, and wheeled me into a special Medi-Van for the trip home. I want to tell you, there was one hell of a big party at the Stingleys all weekend. Tina was there. The boys were there. My mother was there. Friends and neighbors dropped in and out every five minutes. It was a wild time. A happy time. The happiest time of all.

"Let's not overdo it," I said to my family. "The doctors said that if I came through this weekend okay, they'd let me come home every so often for the next few months, just to get accustomed to life on the outside." The way I looked at it, the less time I spent in the Rehab Institute, the better for me.

Just before I went back to the Rehab that weekend, I watched the Patriots play Houston in the AFC wild-card playoff game at Foxborough. The Patriots had finished the season with an 11–5 record, and they had the home-field advantage. Not many people gave them a chance against the Oilers though. And it was not because Houston's Earl Campbell was too much running back for any team to handle.

The Patriots were a team in ruins. Three weeks earlier rumors had begun to spread that Chuck Fairbanks was going to ditch the Patriots as soon as the season ended and take a job as the head football coach at the University of Colorado. Chuck kept denying it, but then it was confirmed that he had talked to the people at

Colorado and indeed was going to take the job there. When this happened, Billy Sullivan got upset, to say the least—who could blame him?—and wouldn't let Chuck coach the final game of the season, a Monday night football special that the Patriots lost to Miami. Billy reinstated Chuck for the playoffs, but the whole Fairbanks mess had the Patriots so screwed up mentally that it seemed likely they'd get blown away by the Oilers.

Which is exactly what happened. Almost before you could say Earl Campbell—and, brother, did the TV announcers say his name a lot, like "Earl Campbell just ran over three Patriots for that first down" and "Earl Campbell just gained another twelve yards" —the Oilers had a three-touchdown lead and routed the Patriots 31–14. The score was a lot closer than the game.

The one thing I'll never forget about watching that game on TV is the sight of Fairbanks walking off the field and the fans in the stands throwing programs and beer cans and everything else at him. I had been with Chuck in 1973 when he launched his program to make Super Bowl champions of the Patriots, and I realized that what I was watching on my TV set was the end of the dream—for Fairbanks, for Billy Sullivan, for the Patriots players, for everyone in New England. And for Number 84, too. Darryl Stingley. I was still a Patriot in my heart and mind. Now the Fairbanks era was over. It should have ended in some other way, with Chuck being carried off the field with the Super Bowl trophy in his hands, not getting pelted with debris by the fans. His own fans.

Once we were into the New Year at the Rehab Institute, things went well every day. Best of all, the horrible and painful bedsores that I'd developed in California were beginning to go away because I was no longer spending most of my time in bed. The sores, which had started off being the size of bottlecaps, had eventually grown to the size of my hand. In fact, for the first few months I was at the Rehab I wasn't allowed to use the therapy pool with the other patients for fear that they'd acquire my infection. So I'd be the last person in the pool each day—alone except for a therapist —and when I was finished, they'd have to pour bottles of disinfectant into the water to clean it up.

"Darryl," a therapist said to me one day, "you're a water polluter."

"Tell me about it," I said.

I became more cheerful than I'd been, and I had been cheerful for some time. I read the Bible all the time, too. You know, most of the prophets didn't want to be prophets; they were just chosen. It made me think. "Darryl, God has chosen you, hand-picked you. This whole thing, your quadriplegia, was meant to be. You're not a victim, Darryl. You're one of His chosen few."

And all the time I was in the Rehab my celebrity was definitely a help. As I moved around in my Medi-Cline chair, I saw patients a lot worse off than I. I was in a private room, not a large ward. I had private nurses at my beck and call. I had the best of everything. Why? Not because I was Darryl Stingley, a truck driver from the South Side who'd been hit by an eighteen-wheeler. I was Darryl Stingley, Number 84, New England Patriots—and so everything was first class all the way. I remember one day I was on an elevator, and another quad looked at my braces and said, "Man, those are great braces. I bet they cost a lot of money." His words stunned me. I really hadn't given all that much thought to the cost of the braces on my arms. To me, they were just braces.

I was indeed a lucky person in many ways. If what happened to me had to be, it sure happened at the right time in my life. As a professional player I was in a situation where unlimited resources were available to me and probably always would be. I didn't lack for anything at the Rehab Institute.

One thing I do regret, looking back, is that I never took the time to develop friendships with any of the other patients at the Rehab. But I was so immersed in myself, in getting to know the new Darryl—Darryl the quad—that I never got around to talking much to other patients. They'd go sit around the lounge in their chairs and tell stories and crack jokes and compare their treatments, but I'd never join them. I was in my own little world, and there was no room in it for anyone else.

The days and the nights passed quickly and almost uneventfully for the next few weeks, and then one day in April, almost six months to the day after I had first entered the Rehab Institute, I went home for good.

"Darryl," I thought on the ride home in the Medi-Van, "you are the one who flew over the cuckoo's nest."

7 · You Can't Go—I Need You

On April 7, 1979, I arrived home at my apartment on Ashland Street, just west of the Loop. I came in almost in the middle of Derek's eighth birthday party. I was convinced that my mind, if not my body, was together, all together, and I was looking forward to a never-ending time of peace and quiet; to being a father; to getting my situation with Tina worked out in the best way for both of us—which, to me, meant getting married sometime soon; to being a productive member of society, an individual whom people in the neighborhood, people everywhere, could look up to and admire. That was my dream, but within days I knew it wasn't going to work.

Right off, Tina and I were at each other's throats morning, noon, and night. She picked on every little thing I did or didn't do. It seemed to me that she just wanted to create arguments, to get my dander up.

"That stereo's so loud it's drivin' me crazy," she'd say. So I'd turn it down.

163

"Will you move your chair away from the table so I can get it cleaned up?" I'd move my chair.

"Darryl, you spilled that milk all over yourself." Big deal. I couldn't help it. But I quickly reached the point where I couldn't stand her nagging any longer. It certainly didn't help that questions were starting to pop up in my mind about our basic relationship.

"Tina's a young and attractive woman," I would say to myself. "Wonder what she was doing when I wasn't around? Hmm, wonder what she does when she leaves the house every day now?"

I knew that in terms of my physical stature, I was an inferior human being, and, well, I didn't know how much I'd be able to do to satisfy Tina sexually. I didn't have much, if any, confidence in myself.

Unfortunately, I made all of my thoughts very plain to her, and that didn't help matters. I got too nasty for my own good. What I should have done was kept my mouth shut and my thoughts to myself. I should have reminded myself that if this woman loved me as she said, then everything would be all right. If she didn't, then there wasn't anything I could do about it. The only thing I could do was wait and see.

In the back of my mind was a thought I had the good sense not to bring up: Maybe I had become something Tina couldn't handle, at least not on a daily basis. I convinced myself that Tina had thought I'd be institutionalized for the rest of my life and that she'd just have to visit me for an hour or so every day. Now, suddenly, here I was in her home—my home—again, and it was too tough for her. So she took her frustrations out on me any way she could.

Not helping the situation at all was the presence of my mother. As the old saying goes, there isn't room for two women—any two women—in the same kitchen.

"I can't stand your mother being here all the time," Tina would tell me. "She's driving me crazy. She's driving the boys crazy. And she'll be driving you crazy in no time at all, too." I knew my mother, knew how she always tried to dominate people with her mind games, and I could understand Tina's problem. She wanted me for herself. At the same time my mother wanted me for herself—the way any mother wants her stricken child. "You know, Darryl," I said to myself, "there's too much selfishness around here on all sides."

Trouble was, I was caught in the middle. I didn't know what I could do to help Tina, other than to jump out of my chair and start walking again, and I didn't know how to cope with my mother. I had enough problems of my own just trying to get accustomed to my new environment. The last thing I needed was the responsibility of being a referee.

One night before dinner Tina and my mother had another one of their battle royals. The next morning when I woke up, Tina said she wanted to talk to me—alone. I could tell from the look in her eyes that she didn't want to exchange any lovey-dovey small talk. Her eyes were blazing. I had a private-duty nurse working full time for me in those days, and I asked her if she'd leave us alone for a little while. She left the room, and it was Tina and me—just the way she wanted it.

"Darryl, I'm leavin'," she said. "And I'm takin' the boys with me. I'm goin' back to my family's place. I can't stand it here anymore. I've got to get away from your mother. Far away. It's not working now, and it won't work as long as she's here." I started to cry. Her words had hit me where it hurt.

"But Tina," I said, "you can't go . . . I need you. And I need the boys. I need all of you. Life's not worth living without the three of you being here with me all the time."

"I understand that, Darryl," Tina said, "but it's no good for us this way. No good. We're not livin' the way things are now. We're just goin' from day to day, waiting for the next big eruption. It's not gonna work." I tried to talk her out of leaving, but it was no use. "I've made my mind up," she said, "and I'm not going to change it."

Then she left to pack.

"Darryl," I said to myself, "there's one way you could get Tina to stay here. But how do you tell your mother that she's got to move out and move out now?" I didn't have that answer. I was caught between a rock and a hard place.

While I was still trying to sort out my thoughts, Hank and Derek came into the room. Both of them were crying, and I began to cry again. "Daddy, we don't want to go," Hank said. "We don't want to leave you here all alone. Daddy, we want to stay with you." I couldn't talk for several minutes. We were all crying. Then Hank picked up a towel and came over to my bed and wiped the tears from my face. "Daddy," he said, "please tell her we don't want to go . . . we want to stay here with you."

"I know you do," I said, the words coming out very slowly. "I know you want to stay here with me. And I want you to stay. I don't want you guys ever to be away from me. We've been apart too much as it is. I thought everything would be perfect for us once I got out of the Rehab and came home, but it hasn't been that way. So, what's happenin' now with your mother and me probably's the best thing for everyone. She's not happy the way things are around here now, and if she's not happy, then I'm not happy. And there's no sense having you guys be unhappy because we're not happy. Know what I mean?"

The boys were crying again, but both were nodding their heads.

"Daddy," Hank said, "we're not gonna go very far, and we're gonna come here and see you all the time." Hank came over and kissed me, and then Derek did the same thing. We were all crying and couldn't stop.

"C'mon, guys," I finally said, "we've all got to act like big men now, don't we? Let's not have your mother see you crying."

"But Daddy," Hank said, "you're gonna be here all alone."

"No, I'm not," I said. "You guys are always gonna be with me because I'm gonna be thinking about you all the time. And that's all I really need to get better. I just need to think about you guys. I live for you guys . . . the two of you. I don't know if we'll ever get to do a lot of things together—you know, like play football and go to games and all that stuff—but we're gonna be together a lot and that will keep me going. I'm proud of you both, proud of the way you've grown up and become little men while I've been sort of out of touch. I'm not gonna let you guys down. I'm gonna keep fighting and keep getting better. And someday we're all gonna be together again."

"The sooner the better," Hank said.

The tears started up all around once again.

I never felt worse in my life, not even when I was in my hospital bed in California with that halo screwed into my head. I never dreamed that I'd ever be saying good-bye to my boys. To me, having them around was going to be the best part of my rehabilitation at home, something to keep me going when times were tough. Now they were leaving. "This place . . . my whole life . . . is going to be empty without them," I thought.

Tina came into the room and told the boys that it was time to go. Hank kissed me again, and so did Derek. I couldn't control myself and was crying like anything.

"It's okay, Dad," Hank said. "We're coming back to see you all the time."

"I know you will," I said.

And then they were gone.

I slumped into my chair and began to cry again. God, what had I done to deserve this? Hadn't I suffered enough already? Life was the pits, the worst. I cried myself to sleep that night and every night for the next few weeks. But all the crying couldn't ease my pain. I was a man alone. A crippled man alone. It was me against the world. Or so it seemed. And it was awful.

Every night I'd lie in my bed flat on my back and think about Tina and why she had left. I came to the conclusion that Tina had just said to herself, "What can I do with a man like that?"—and when she couldn't come up with a satisfactory answer, she moved out. That was her answer: to abandon me. If she had asked me that same question, my answer would have been: "Well, what is it you think a man should be?" I suppose it sounds funny to answer a question with a question, but my life was becoming one big question.

When Tina left and took the boys with her, everyone in my family acted shocked. Really shocked.

"I always knew Tina'd pull something like this," my mother said. "But we'll take care of you, Darryl. We'll take good care of you. You're one of us." And they did. Harold came by to help me get into bed at night. Wayne kept me posted on all the happenings in the world of sports and kept freshening up my record supply with the latest hits. And Andrea played her big-sister role to perfection, doing little things whenever I asked—or didn't ask. My mother was both sympathetic and sensitive, and didn't get herself all worked up over seeing her son confined to his wheelchair or to his bed.

But those good days seemed to last only a few months.

The people at the Rehab Institute had always preached independence to me, and they were continuing to preach the doctrine during my regular visits as an outpatient. I wanted to be as independent as possible, too. I wanted to do even more than the therapists had programmed. My family was supposed to be encouraging me in that regard, but instead, it seemed to be doing the opposite. The way I saw it, they were flat out refusing to encourage me to go beyond my limits, to strive for a higher level of independence. They were letting me down, and it hurt.

For instance, I'd say, "I'm gonna take a trip down to the lobby for an hour."

"No, no, that's too much for you today," my mother or somebody else in the family would say. "You'd better stay here with us."

Thanks to the Patriots, I had bought a van specially outfitted to

One of Purdue's greatest stars, Darryl ranked sixth in all-time career receptions (69); third in reception yards (1256); third in single season reception yards (734 in 1971). *(Photo courtesy of Boilermaker Sports Information.)*

The 1973 first round draft choices: John Hannah, from Alabama; coach Fairbanks; Darryl; Sam Cunningham, from USC.
(Photo courtesy of New England Patriots.)

Displaying the incredible height and reach for which he became famous.
(Photo courtesy Thomas J. Croke.)

In full stride against the Falcons. *(Photo courtesy of Thomas J. Croke.)*

Scoring against the Raiders in 1976. George Atkinson looks on in anguish. *(Photo courtesy of Dick Raphael and the New England Patriots.)*

John Madden.

Returning to Foxboro on October 14, 1979, Darryl spends time with an old friend—Russ Francis.
(*Photo courtesy of Thomas J. Croke.*)

Darryl receiving the International Award for Valor in Sport. February, 1980. *(Photo courtesy Wide World Photos.)*

The new Executive Director of Player Personnel for the New England Patriots. *(Photo courtesy of Thomas J. Croke.)*

Scoring once more against Oakland.

(Photos courtesy of Thomas J. Croke.)

handle quads, complete with hydraulic lifts and all kinds of security systems to keep my chair and me locked into position while the van was in motion. Harold had even installed a fantastic stereo system in it for me. The van was easy to operate, and I was eager to have my friends come by and take me out for drives. My family didn't like that.

"A friend of mine is taking me downtown to a club tonight and we're going to listen to some music," I announced one morning.

"Oh no you're not." And when my friend came by to get me that night, my mother was waiting for him outside the door to tell him that I'd come down with a cold and wouldn't be able to go out with him.

"Darryl," my mother said, "we're just trying to protect you. We're lookin' out for your best interests."

"No you're not," I said. "You're being overprotective. I know what my best interests are. They're my independence and my development as a new person. Staying around here and doing nothing isn't helping me. I've got to get out and be with people, with my friends, can't you understand that?"

They couldn't.

My mother and I always seemed to be at war. In public, everything between us always appeared cheery and rosy. In private, though, everything was hell. I looked at my mother as someone who desperately wanted to gain control over my life.

One night I had a bunch of friends and their ladies up to the apartment to listen to some music and have a few cool ones. Remember, I was paying the rent, the food bills, the phone bills, everything. No sooner had we gotten comfortable than my mother said to my friends, "Why are you here? You're in the way, get out."

Finally they got fed up and left.

What my mother wanted, I thought, was for people to regard her as a martyr. She was always able to use me as her excuse when the situation wasn't right for her. For instance, the phone would ring. "Hello?" my mother'd say. There'd be a pause of a few moments, and then my mother'd say, "Why thank you, but you know I can't leave my Darryl. Tina left him, you know, and I'm stayin' here with him all the time. I'm the only one he's got left to take care of him." I'd get mad as hell and shout and holler at her and tell her to go out, but it never did me any good.

Then there'd come a situation that was right for her, and the whole scene was different: The phone would ring. "Hello?" my mother'd say. There'd be a pause, a long pause, and then my mother'd say, "Why thank you, I'd love to be there." Then she'd hang up the phone and say to me, "I'm goin' out tonight, so you'd better get one of your friends over here to help take care of you."

She straddled both sides of the fence pretty well.

One night I started to talk about the situation to Andrea, but my mother kept butting in and trying to keep me from getting a word in. Everytime I said something to Andrea about my situation, my mother'd say, "Don't believe him. He's lyin', he's lyin'."

"Okay, I'm lyin'," I said. "But you people want me to be a zero, and you're telling people that I'm a zero. To you, I'm deaf, dumb, and blind, as well as a quadriplegic. Home has been hell for me. I've cried more here than I ever did anywhere else. You people— my own people, my own family, my own flesh and blood—never stop trying to mess with my head. I understood it when the doctors and the therapists played their mind games with me, but why are you people trying to play those games. Hardly a day's gone by that I haven't felt totally rejected and abandoned."

Andrea looked at me and started to cry.

"Andrea," I said, "I'm a nobody among my own people. Out there in the street people think I'm a somebody. But I don't get that feeling from my own family. Out in the street people think I represent something. Andrea, I'm a nobody to my family because I'm not doin' what they want me to do when they want me to do it. Can't they understand? I'm alive, not dead. Give me a break."

That same night I had a long argument with my mother about

finances. I had gotten a bill for the insurance on my van and was going to have my secretary pay it. (I had hired a part-time secretary to answer my mail, pay the bills, and look after my overall business affairs.)

"Can I please have that insurance bill?" I said to my mother as she was going through the mail. That was all she needed to hear.

"You don't trust me," she said, flying off the handle. "I'm your mother, and you don't trust me. You think I'm out for myself, don't you. You think I don't care about you. Well, you're wrong, Darryl, and someday you'll realize it!"

What nobody seemed to understand was my sense of total frustration. I'd always been my own person; if something had to be done, I did it myself. Now, for the first time in my life, I was dependent on others for everything—and I was having a tough time handling it.

All this time Tina was mostly an innocent bystander, watching from a safe distance. She came around with the boys about once a week, and when I could get my mother out of the house, we'd have a good rap session. Just about every time I saw Tina, I said to her:

"Are you ready to come back yet?"

"No, not yet," she'd say. And she'd tell me there was no way she could live in the same apartment with my mother—and that was that. Period.

One day when my mother and I were alone, I said to her, "I'm giving serious thought to getting back together with Tina and the boys and doing things the right way from here on in. Tying the knot and everything. So, I'd like you to move out of the apartment so Tina and the boys can move back in." You'd have thought I'd asked her to fly to the moon.

"I'll move when I'm good and ready," she growled. "You don't ask me to move, and you don't tell me to move."

"Okay," I said, "then I'll move." She got a big laugh out of that.

"You're gonna move?" she said. "You? Where you gonna go?

179

Who's gonna take care of you? Listen, you're not goin' nowhere."
That night I heard her on the telephone talking to a friend. "The
funniest thing happened today," she said. "Darryl told me he's
going to move."

Maybe it was funny to her, but it wasn't funny to me. My
mother didn't hear me the next day when I was on my squawk-box
phone with my lawyer in Boston, Jack Sands.

"Jack, I've got to move."

"Probably not a bad idea," he said. "Where do you want to go?
New England? The warm weather?"

"I've thought about moving to New England and living close to
Foxborough," I said, "and I've thought about Arizona and Florida
and California. But they're not right as long as Tina and I haven't
worked things out. I don't want to get that far from my boys. I've
decided I ought to buy a house or a condominium somewhere in
Chicago and have the interior modified so a handicapped person
can live in it easily. You know, wider doorways, therapy pool,
special lighting and all that stuff. I think it'd be perfect for me."

"You're right, Darryl," Jack said. "But it's not something we
should jump into. It'll take time to do it right."

"I know that," I told him. "I just wanted you to know what I'm
thinking. Everything around her is so damn depressing that I'm
just looking for something positive to think about."

In a strange, and illuminating, way my difficulties with Tina and
my family ultimately marked the beginning of another life for me.
I had a deep feeling of rejection, of abandonment, and I felt on the
verge of total depression. Never had I been so down. Not when I
was fighting for my life at Eden Hospital. Not when I was struggling to establish my first new self at the Rehab Institute.

I think that what follows depression in most cases is death, and
on many occasions I felt that death would have been the better
way for me, certainly better than being treated like a worthless
nobody, which was the way I felt at home.

One night in the summer of 1979 I asked my Uncle Ed Brown to take me downtown and stay with me in a hotel for a couple of nights so I could get some peace and quiet—things I could never get at home—and have some meetings with Jack Sands, to discuss my financial future.

I was in a room on one of the upper floors, looking out over Lake Michigan, and after dinner my first night I moved my chair almost against the window—which ran almost floor to ceiling and opened onto a tiny ledge—and gazed out at the city. The lights were bright, the sky was clear. A perfect night for romance . . . or death.

"Darryl," I said to myself, "you could take yourself out of your misery in just about two seconds. All you have to do is push the switch on the chair forward and you'll go right through the window." It was a chilling, haunting thought. But not for me. I jolted my chair into reverse and crashed into a chair, knocking it over and also knocking over a table and light. Uncle Ed was in the next room with my nurse and some other friends who had joined us for dinner, and when he heard the commotion he charged through the door to see what was happening.

"Darryl, Darryl, you all right?" he said, his voice filled with alarm.

"Everything's fine, Uncle Ed, everything's just fine," I said. "Just got my finger stuck on the button."

In my head, everything suddenly was fine. At least for the moment. I wouldn't give up. I wouldn't let them get to me. I wouldn't drive my chair through any window. I'd fight 'em. I'd fight for my life, and I'd fight for it any way I had to. It would be me against them, if that's the way they wanted it. That's the way it had been at the Rehab Institute, and I'd do it again.

When I returned to Ashland Street after meeting with Jack I brought a completely new attitude with me. My mother or anyone else in the family could say what they wanted and do what they wanted, but I wouldn't let it get me down. I'd do my own thing in my own good sweet time. And if they didn't like it, that was too bad. Almost immediately I started to go out more and more. I'd go

181

to baseball games, discos, parties, anywhere. I never had any trouble finding friends to take me places in my van, day or night.

Then one day, early in August, I got a call from Jack Sands in Boston.

"Darryl," he said, "the Patriots open the season with a Monday night TV game against Pittsburgh on Labor Day, which is September third. They'd like you to fly here and be at the game."

"What do you think, Jack?"

"It'd be the best thing in the world for you," he said.

"Jack, tell 'em I'll be there." And that's all I thought about for the next few weeks—going back to New England and seeing all my old teammates. Leon Gray. Russ Francis. Sam (Bam) Cunningham. Prentice McCray. Tony McGee. Everyone. It was going to be a hot time in the old town when I got there.

But first I had a decision to make.

8 · Get the Game Goin' Again!

For months Jack Sands and I had wrestled with the question of whether or not to take legal action against the National Football League, its twenty-eight member clubs and one Jack Tatum and sue them for the exact figure of $87 million on our claim that collectively and individually they had permitted and encouraged and performed the type of violence and assault that led to my injury on the field that night in Oakland.

An alternative, as Jack had plainly outlined, was to reach an out-of-court settlement with the NFL and accept an annual cash payout that would, when combined with various Social Security and workmen's compensation benefits, not only cover all my expenses as long as I live, but also provide for the welfare of Tina and my sons and their future educational needs.

Now it was approaching decision time, because California, the state where I would have to file suit, had a one-year statute of limitations in matters of assault and injury. That meant I'd have to make up my mind—suit or settlement?—by August 12, 1979, the anniversary of the hit.

It was not an easy decision.

Jack had done his homework well. He felt the courts and juries in California would be sympathetic and in the end would award me at least several million in damages.

"It's all there on the game films and in pictures," he told me. "There's no way in the world that Tatum, or anyone else, will be able to convince a judge and a jury that his actions when he hit you weren't premeditated assault with intent to injure. In our society, you just don't do to someone—on the field or off—what Tatum did to you and get away with it."

But did I want to sue the NFL? I didn't think so. And I don't believe Jack thought I should sue either.

True, Jack Tatum deserved to be dragged into a courtroom and made to explain once and for all what he had done to me. It was almost a year since he had put me down for good, and I still had not heard one word from him. Not one word. The least he could have done was visit me at the hospital in Oakland, or send his best wishes for my recovery along with those of his Raider teammates who did take the time and make the effort to see me at the hospital. But no, Jack Tatum apparently couldn't do that, and that told me a lot about Jack Tatum.

True, I didn't have any great feeling for Pete Rozelle, the Commissioner of the National Football League, the number one man in the game. As far as I knew, Rozelle hadn't called me in the hospital, either. That told me a lot about Pete Rozelle.

True, the game itself was suffering from an overdose of violence, and there were more cheap-shot artists running around than ever before. But at the same time, football was my game. I loved it. I played it. And I still wanted to be involved in it in some way in the future. In fact, as soon as I possibly could.

A suit against the NFL and Jack Tatum might indeed make me a lot of money and give me the financial security I needed to make it through life and my boys needed to make it through college, but

I'd have to spend five or six years running from one California court to another—and, hey, I couldn't run anymore.

Sure, I'd win all the sympathy votes every time I'd be wheeled into a courtroom in my chair, and the TV networks would cover the case, and the newspapers and newsmagazines would be there, but that wasn't what I wanted. I wasn't a publicity seeker. The fact of the matter was that I really didn't blame football itself. My bitterness was directed at Jack Tatum, because when he played the game of football, to my mind it wasn't within the spirit of the rules that governed everyone else's conduct on the field.

In the back of my mind, too, was something that Chuck Sullivan (Billy's son, who, among other things, was the executive vice-president of the Patriots) had said shortly after it became clear that I had taken my last step. Chuck was talking on the phone with Jack Sands, when he said "Darryl will not have to worry about anything for the rest of his life, we'll make sure of that." So I called Jack one day and suggested that he see what type of settlement the NFL would be interested in making. The bottom line was financial security, that's all. I had no interest in being a millionaire courtesy of the courts. Jack thought it was the right approach.

"Yeah," I said, "but if we can't work out a proper settlement, one that gives me the security I need, we'll have to take them to court."

Jack immediately contacted Billy Sullivan and arranged a meeting to open discussions about a settlement. At their first meeting Billy said to Jack, "We want to do what's best for Darryl. In the NFL there is an unwritten law from Pete Rozelle that every team must keep its own house in order regarding the settlement of injury matters. Darryl is a Patriot, and we'll take care of him."

Billy Sullivan appointed his son Chuck to negotiate a possible settlement with Jack and me. Actually, Chuck and Jack did all the hard talking, and I did all the listening when Jack called me at the Rehab Institute or my apartment to tell me how he was making

185

out in his discussions. The first time he called, he didn't sound too optimistic.

"I think it's going to be long and drawn out, and we may not be able to reach a settlement before the filing date for a suit," Jack said. "Every time I made a suggestion to Chuck about future financial arrangements, he'd say to me, 'Jack, I'll have to get back to you on that.' Darryl, you know what that means, don't you?"

What that meant, or at least what I thought it meant, was that the Patriots had to clear all discussions with Rozelle and the NFL's legal experts.

We went round and round for several months. The Patriots weren't devious or anything, they just had to make certain that what they did was what the NFL wanted them to do. As we got closer and closer to the filing deadline, the NFL began to come around to our way of thinking—which really didn't surprise me.

For some unknown reason, no penalty had been called against Jack Tatum on the play in which I was injured. And the films and pictures that Jack Sands had collected sure seemed to show that Tatum's hit on me was in no way legal by NFL standards—or any other standards. Sands and I had felt all along that the last thing the NFL wanted was for a courtroom to be shown game films and blowups of still picture sequences of my hit—with me sitting there in my chair, taking it all in—and then be asked to decide if what Tatum had done to me was legal. No way the NFL wanted its game officials dragged into court to explain Tatum's actions or their own failure to drop a flag and call a penalty.

At last, just a few days before my August 12, 1979, filing deadline, the Patriots presented their—and the NFL's—final settlement offer. Jack relayed the proposal to me and told me to read it carefully and think about it for several days. Which I did. Then Jack called me one morning to give me his own reaction to the offer.

"Let me just say this, Darryl," Jack said, "and maybe it will help in your decision, although maybe you've made it already. I think what the Patriots and the NFL have offered is very fair by any standards. You might get a helluva lot more money down the road from a jury, but it would be a long way down the road and I, for one, don't know if you ever want to make that trip."

The settlement was fair, as Jack said. I wasn't by any means going to get rich, but I'd be able to live comfortably and provide for Tina and the boys—and the boys would be able to get their education even if I died. My bottom line—financial security— was being met.

"I agree with everything you say," I replied to Jack. "It all seems fine to me. The only thing that bothers me is that it lets Jack Tatum off the hook, and he doesn't deserve to escape so easily. But the good things outnumber the bad, and I think I ought to take their offer."

"So do I," Jack said.

The decision was made. Settlement, not suit.

One of the terms of the agreement between the Patriots and me was that neither party would ever divulge the financial arrangements. I can say, though, that the settlement was strictly a settlement of injuries, which meant that the money I'd be receiving each month would be tax-free. Also, under the terms of the agreement, I agreed not to take any future legal action against the NFL in the matter of the injury I had sustained in Oakland. Which meant, of course, that I also couldn't sue Jack Tatum for damages on the grounds of assault, because a suit against Tatum would necessarily involve the NFL. All in all, it was not the best of worlds, but not the worst either.

And so the next stop on my schedule—the first real stop since my injury—was New England and the opening game of the 1979 NFL season between the Patriots and the Super Bowl Champion Pittsburgh Steelers.

As I made my final arrangements for the trip to Boston, I had very mixed emotions. At one point, in fact, I wanted to cancel the whole trip and stay home in Chicago and just watch the game on television. I thought that the trip might be too much for me. Sure, I was eagerly awaiting the first reunion with my Patriot teammates since the night they visited me at the hospital in Oakland after beating the Raiders. Many of them had faithfully kept in contact. Sam Cunningham had dropped by to see me on his way home from New England to California after the 1978 season. Stanley Morgan had flown out from New England to see me, and he had been sending me plants and flowers regularly with all sorts of get-well-quick messages. I wanted to see Russ Francis, Tony McGee, and Prentice McCray, three of the other Patriots who came by to see me in Chicago, and everyone else. It was going to be a great homecoming, no doubt about it.

At the same time, I knew it was going to be a media event. I knew Billy Sullivan and his love of publicity, and I knew he'd try to get maximum exposure for the game. There would be press conferences and more press conferences. The ABC Monday Night Football crew would be there—and that meant Howard Cosell. And that meant Howard would have a chance to reflect on the entire matter of one Darryl Stingley for the ABC audience: the hit, Jack Tatum, my condition, the settlement—everything.

On top of that, the Patriots would be playing their first game under their new head coach, Ron (Fargo) Erhardt, who had moved up from offensive coordinator following "Chuck Fairbanks's big-bucks defection to the University of Colorado," as all the Boston papers put it every day. It would be the highlight of Fargo's career—his debut as an NFL head coach against the defending Super Bowl champions—and frankly I didn't know if I should be horning in on his show.

And of course there was the question of getting to Boston in the first place. When you're a quadriplegic, you don't just ring up an airline and reserve a seat or two on some flight from Chicago to Boston. And when you get to Boston or wherever, you just don't grab a cab to the hotel, hop up the escalator to the check-in counter, zip up to your room, take a shower, and then get on with your activities. I doubt that even the staff of the President of the United States has to make as many arrangements for a trip as I do. I needed two first-class seats (in my condition I can't fly coach) one with a special seat belt and neck harness so I'd remain secure during flight; a Medi-Van in Boston, so I could travel about in my chair; and a nurse on call throughout my stay in New England. I also needed a place to go for therapy, so I wouldn't backslide on my physical-exercise programs. You name it, I needed it.

One afternoon I called Jack Sands to tell him about my concerns, that maybe I wasn't ready to make such a trip yet.

"Whaddya mean, Darryl," Jack said. "Claudia Smith's (the Patriots' director of public affairs) got everything all arranged. And you know Claudia, too, so you know that everything'll be just perfect while you're here. All you've got to do is get to O'Hare and get on the plane. Everything else's all taken care of. And you're going to be treated like a king once you get here."

My worries were gradually being erased. I knew Claudia, and she'd do everything right. Then Jack came through with the clincher.

"What nobody's mentioned to you so far, Darryl," he said, "is that we're planning to have a lobster dinner waiting for you in your hotel room when you get here."

"That does it," I said. "I'm coming."

I delayed my arrival in Boston until almost the last minute, because I didn't want to disturb my teammates—I still considered them to be teammates, because I was one of them in spirit, if not in body—as they prepared to play the Steelers on Labor Day. I also decided I wouldn't visit with any of the Patriots until after the game was over, just as they had not visited me until after the game in Oakland. First things first.

A couple of hours before the game I was having dinner at Foxborough with Jack Sands, when we got a call from Billy Sullivan.

"Darryl," Billy said, "I've got one big favor to ask of you. I've just had dinner with Howard Cosell, and it would mean a lot to me, to all the Sullivans, and to the entire Patriots family if you'd have a few words with Howard on national television."

I knew where Billy was coming from, but even so, I was stunned. When Jack told the Patriots I didn't want my visit to be turned into a media circus, Billy had mentioned that he felt the same way. No interviews on national television. No dog-and-pony show for Howard Cosell. In fact, Howard's daughter, Hillary Cosell, who worked for NBC-TV, had been pressing Jack to let her do the first national TV interview with me, and one of her arguments to Jack was that she'd do it better than her father because she wouldn't turn it into a circus.

Jack took the phone to talk to Billy.

"Billy," he said, "I thought this was the last thing the Patriots wanted, Darryl talking with Cosell."

Billy told Jack of his long friendship with Cosell, and said that Howard would be sympathetic toward Darryl. Billy also said he thought the interview would be a good thing for the Patriots.

Now I was really torn. I didn't know what was going on, but I decided I'd do the interview with Cosell anyway. I thought it would be harmless.

Before the game I had Jack go to a meeting with the ABC people to make sure that the interview would be handled aboveboard and in a professional manner. Dr. Birkenfeld was at the meeting, too, giving the ABC people some insight into the type of questions they should avoid. ABC had some things to ask Dr. Birkenfeld, and he handled the medical questions without any problem. Then ABC got into some nonmedical areas, and Dr. Birkenfeld turned the conference over to Jack.

All eyes turned to him, and suddenly Cosell, who hadn't said a word in twenty minutes—that had to be a world record for Howard—and who had never even met Jack before, asked him, "Hey, Kid, how much is in this for you? What's your cut on this guy?"

Jack was enraged, and rightfully so. "Mr. Cosell," he said, "my fee arrangement is between my client and myself, and I resent your line of questioning."

Cosell snickered, and then he said, "I understand that you and Howard Slusher are going into business together."

Now, Jack was madder than ever. Howard Slusher was the agent from Los Angeles who had advised John Hannah and Leon Gray to stay away from practices and games in 1977 until the Patriots renegotiated their contracts; the Sullivans and most other NFL owners probably considered Slusher their number one enemy in the agent/attorney field.

"Mr. Cosell," Jack said, "I've never met Howard Slusher in my life."

At that point Cosell gave his usual cackle and turned away to talk to some other ABC people.

When Jack came out of that room, madder than hell, and told me what had happened inside, I could only say, "Jack, welcome to the Wide World of Monday Night Football." Jack assured me that the agreement was that I'd appear with Cosell before the game, and we'd tape an interview that would run at halftime. The interview would be brief and it would not be provocative. But almost immediately I began to think about it. Not think, really, but worry. I dreaded Cosell had something up his sleeve for me, something I wouldn't be able to cope with on my own terms at that moment.

And then the ABC cameras were on me, and Cosell was speaking to America.

Howard was very somber as he told the story of my injury, my hospitalization, my rehabilitation, and my present situation. He said that he and everyone admired me for the way I had battled against my quadriplegia, and he said that it was "remarkable" how far I'd come. I distinctly remember him saying that word— "remarkable."

I was nervous and didn't know what to say, so I didn't say very

191

much. In fact, the whole interview went by so fast that I don't remember what I said on TV.

Then, as I feared, Howard caught me by surprise. He said, recalling his exact words as best I can: "Today, Darryl Stingley signed a contract with the New England Patriots to be their executive director of player personnel for the rest of his life. And, Darryl, isn't it a wonderful thing what the Patriots and the Sullivan family have done for you?"

I looked at Cosell; I had no idea what he was talking about. I knew what the Sullivans had done for me and all the background to it, but I didn't know about any contract I had signed to be the executive director of player personnel. In fact, the Patriots had never discussed any such thing with Jack or me. I was at a loss for words.

Cosell finished the interview by linking Walter O'Malley, the owner of the Brooklyn–Los Angeles Dodgers, and Roy Campanella, the great Dodgers' catcher of the late 1940s and 1950s—the way the O'Malley family had taken care of Campanella following the car accident that left him crippled for life—with Billy Sullivan and Darryl Stingley. Then the cameras turned away and the lights went out. As Cosell stood up to go back to his regular seat in the booth, he practically bumped into Jack Sands.

"Wasn't I great, Kid?" he said to Jack.

"Mr. Cosell," Jack said, "who told you that Darryl signed a contract with the Patriots to be their executive director of player personnel?"

"Billy Sullivan told me at dinner last night that they were going to announce it today, that he had signed Darryl to a lifetime agreement."

"Mr.Cosell," Jack said, "that's absolutely untrue. Darryl has signed nothing with the New England Patriots regarding any future employment. There's no agreement between Darryl and the Patriots on anything except a settlement for his injuries."

Howard tried to answer Jack, but Jack cut him off quickly. "Mr. Cosell," he said, "what I resent most is your saying that Darryl Stingley has signed anything with anyone, and Darryl resents it as much as I do. Mr. Cosell, Darryl can't sign anything because at this point in his life he cannot even write his name."

That was the last I saw of Howard Cosell.

A few minutes before kickoff I was wheeled into a private booth in the press box and set into a position from which I could watch the game in comfort. I had never seen a game from a press box before, not even when I had been injured, and one thing suddenly hit me: The players down there on the field, guys I knew stood 6 feet 5 inches and weighed 275 pounds, all looked so little, like so many toy soldiers.

The players came onto the field, and the Patriots were given a tremendous ovation by the home crowd of 61,000. Once the game began, I tried to follow the play closely, but I felt lost trying to view the action from such a distance. Both teams seemed to be in midseason, or even postseason, form, and the play was spirited.

Suddenly, without any warning, I heard the announcer mention "Darryl Stingley" and say something to the effect that I was watching the game from a booth in the press box and that everyone should say hello to me. Well, almost as one, those 61,000 fans stood up. They cheered, they waved, they flew white handkerchiefs. On the field itself, the Patriots all waved too, some taking off their helmets so that maybe I'd be able to see their faces. Even the Pittsburgh players joined in and waved to me.

I wanted to wave back, but of course I couldn't.

It was overwhelming. The noise and the waving continued, and continued, for what seemed like forever. All I could see was a sea of 61,000 faces looking up at me. I started to cry. I couldn't hold back the tears. It was too much, much too much, for me to handle. The noise and the waving continued. At one point the referee thought there had been enough sentiment for the night and tried to start the action by blowing his whistle, but nobody heard him. No way the game could resume with all this noise. The quarterbacks would never be heard, not in the huddle, not at the line of scrimmage. It would be total chaos.

Finally, after almost eight minutes, the noise and the waving began to subside, the 61,000 people began to take their seats, and the game started up again. I'll never forget those eight minutes. Never. It's almost as if I can see each and every one of those 61,000 faces right now in my mind. Boy, did that great outpouring boost my spirits. "Darryl," I said to myself, "just imagine what's gonna happen the day you break out of your chair and walk onto that field under your own power. They'll tear the whole stadium down and half the town of Foxborough."

The rest of the night was pretty much of a downer, with the Patriots losing the game in sudden-death overtime. It was so late when it ended, well past 12:30 A.M., that I decided not to visit the locker room, as I had planned. I'd wait until the afternoon to visit my old teammates.

Before my visit the next day, though, Jack had the Patriots arrange a press conference to clarify Cosell's remarks about my supposed new job with the team. Billy Sullivan was very uncomfortable as he sat there listening to Jack state that what Cosell had said on TV was wholly inaccurate, which indeed it was. Billy concurred with Jack's statement. There also was an unofficial apology of sorts from the Patriots.

To clear up this matter: I was named the Patriots' executive director of player personnel shortly after that visit to Boston. However, I did not sign a contract with the Patriots for this job, and I have not been paid to perform it. The Patriots have picked up whatever expenses I have incurred in serving as their executive director of player personnel, mainly travel expenses back and forth from Chicago to Boston, and costs of hotels, transporation, meals, etc., in Boston. For now, the job is more title than anything else, but I hope that someday I will be physically able to work at it on a regular basis, not just at draft time, the way I do now.

When I finally got to meet my old teammates, I felt as though I was in heaven. I went out onto the field in my chair, and it was like being home again, right down on the 50-yard line. For a moment, a brief moment, I could hear the voice of some radio announcer in my head: "Third and long for the Patriots at midfield . . . they're set up flanker right, Stingley on the wide side . . . and Grogan's back to pass . . . he's being rushed hard . . . he rolls to his right . . . he throws . . . there's Stingley down at the ten-yard line . . . he's got it. Oh, what a move Stingley put on number forty-five . . . and he's in the end zone . . . TOUCHDOWN PATRIOTS! TOUCH-DOWN PATRIOTS! Darryl Stingley puts the Patriots in the lead with a fifty-yard touchdown catch from Steve Grogan, and, ladies and gentlemen, did he ever fake that safetyman right out of his shoes." The image was all too fleeting.

One by one my former teammates came by to say their hellos and have some fun, and also to apologize for not having a victory ball to give me the night before.

"Sting," said Stanley Morgan, "we come out to your town next month to play the Bears, and we're gonna have a lot of touchdown balls to give to you and one game ball."

"Promises, promises, Stanley," I said. "All I'm getting from you is promises. I want some footballs—not promises."

Stanley laughed. "Don't worry, you'll get more footballs than you know what to do with."

Shelby Jordan rapped with me for a few minutes, and then I heard him telling one of the members of the press: "Darryl's body may not be strong, but his heart is. I've seen a great many people who couldn't handle difficult times. I know how hard it is to accept things that befall us and how tough it can be to deal with them. I've had difficulties to overcome, but nothing like Darryl's faced. It takes a special kind of person to fight back as hard as Darryl has from an injury as bad as his. He is truly an inspiration. When you see what he's done, how far he's come, you have to be inspired. I have a very special love for Darryl. Just seeing him does a lot for my mental makeup." What can I say?

Russ Francis chatted with me for a couple of moments and let me know that his love life was in its usual condition, which meant A-1.

Steve Grogan also stopped to see me, but I don't really remember what he had to say. A couple of weeks before coming to New England I read a quote of Steve's in the newspaper, and suddenly I began to feel sorry for him. True, I had been critical, and rightly so, of Steve's passing ability. But unbeknownst to me, a lot of people had publicly and privately been blaming him for my injury, and that wasn't right. I know, the pass was over my head, and I was left vulnerable to Tatum's hit, but, hey, half the passes in football go incomplete for one reason or another. They're too high, too low, too wide, you name it. No quarterback's perfect.

What Steve had said in the *Boston Globe* was this:

Darryl's injury has been a difficult thing for me. It's hard for me to put into words what I feel. People have said mean things about me and a columnist wrote mean things—that Darryl's injury was my fault. I've thought about that often. I've tried as best I can to look at both sides of it. I've thrown thousands of passes in my career; high passes, low passes— and perfect passes. In my mind, there's no way to blame myself for what happened, that because the pass was high, Darryl was hurt. Blame me? I don't think so.

I really don't know about this. Anytime you have an injury like this, you have to take a close look at this sport. There are players in this league who will intimidate people every time they get the chance. They feel that intimidating people will make them better players. But there are people who overdo it at times. It's sad to look at it this way, but this is what the American public wants. They want to see people getting hit.

And we're the ones—the football players—who are crazy enough to go out there on the field and do it. We love football. We're the ones who do it.

I wanted to say to Steve, "Hey, it wasn't your fault," but I didn't know how.

I was just getting to feel at home when I had to cut short the visit because my breathing was getting very heavy; I was coming down with another of my many colds.

"See you guys in Chicago next month," I said as I left the stadium.

"Darryl, don't worry," Stanley Morgan said to me, "we'll have some footballs for you."

On that note I departed and, the next day, flew back to Chicago. What a trip it had been! Most of the previous thirteen months had been a downer, one long downer, but the trip to New England had been one great tonic. It was exactly what I had needed. I had been stuffed with clam chowder, New England style, and lobster. I had seen my friends. My spirits were even higher than the plane as I jetted back home. Except for the screw-up with the Cosell interview, it had been a perfect trip.

"You know, Darryl," I said to myself somewhere over London, Ontario, "the world's not such a bad place after all. People aren't out to get you, they're there to help you. You've just got to give them the chance."

I knew I had been pretty rough on some people, particularly my family, but I thought that I had to be that way in order to assert and show my independence the way they had been after me to do down at the Rehab Institute. But the trip to New England had relaxed me, and I promised myself that I'd cool it a bit once I got back home. Oh, I'd still assert my independence, but I'd try to see the other side of things perhaps a little better. Also, I wouldn't be so much of a recluse. With just one or two exceptions, I had refused to meet with sports writers, medical writers, TV reporters or anyone else in the media. I had tried to keep the details of my

197

condition pretty private. But the press in New England had treated me beautifully, like a long-lost son returning from combat, and I saw that my worries about being treated unfairly by the press were unfounded after all. I decided I'd make myself available more often when people from the press wanted to talk to me.

Over the preceding year I had received thousands of letters from others who had been struck down with conditions similar to mine, and I tried to respond to as many of the letter writers as I possibly could. The way I saw it now, the press could help get my message to people with disabilities like mine. I'd use the press to relay my messages of hope, of courage, of conviction. Why not? One story in the papers might be read by a couple of million people.

Back in Chicago, I couldn't wait for October 14, the day the Patriots played the Chicago Bears at Soldier Field. I called George (Papa Bear) Halas, who had been a great friend to me and all the Stingleys ever since I returned from Oakland to Chicago, and told him that I'd probably need a dozen tickets for me and my family.

"No problem," he said, "you can have two dozen if you need 'em."

As it turned out, I needed twenty-three tickets to accomodate all the Stingleys and other friends who accompanied me to the game. I sat down on the field in my chair, and before the game I talked with all the Patriots and a lot of the Bears, and got some hugs and kisses from the Honey Bears.

"If you score a touchdown," I said to Stanley Morgan, "please bring me that ball. I'd really like that."

"You've got it," Stanley said.

The game was barely three minutes old when Stanley beat Virgil Livers in the corner and pulled in a Grogan pass for a touchdown. The moment he scored, Stanley started to wave the ball high in his right hand.

"Come to poppa," I kept saying on the sidelines. "Come to

poppa." And that's what Stanley did. He brought that ball right to me.

Before the game I had told Russ Francis that from watching the Bears' games all season I knew their safeties like to blitz more than they should; as a result, the middle often would be open for a deep pass. Sure enough, Grogan beat the safety blitzers on one play with a long touchdown bomb to Harold Jackson—and another football ended up in my lap.

"That was Darryl's call all the way," Francis told the press after the game when the matter of Jackson's touchdown reception came up. "He had been talking to us about how that pass would be open just before we went onto the field. They blitzed, and there it was. Touchdown. Just the way Darryl said it would be." Just call me Coach Stingley.

The Patriots went on to win by 27–7, so I had a lot of footballs to take home, including the game ball, which Hank and Derek used to play touch football while I went into the victor's locker room.

It was a beautiful day, but like all beautiful days it had to end. I said my good-byes to the Patriots as they headed for the bus that would take them to the airport for the flight back to New England. It was not so much a good-bye as a "Be seein' you again soon" type of farewell.

At home, the days and the nights became almost interchangeable. I was still having family problems and there was no progress to report with Tina, but my trip to Boston and my travels around Chicago had proved to all of them that I wasn't going to spend the rest of my life cooped up in an apartment. I was going to live life as fully as I could, not bound by geographical restrictions, financial restrictions, or anything else. I was in the early stages of my new life.

A couple of months later, toward the end of the NFL season, my spirits, which, all things considered, had been pretty high, suddenly took an unexpected tumble.

The phone rang in my apartment.

"Darryl there please?" Jack Sands said to my therapist, who answered the phone.

"Hold on a second, please." The therapist turned on my squawk box, so I could hear Jack and talk to him without having the receiver on my shoulder.

"Hey, Jack, Merry Christmas," I said to him.

"Darryl," Jack said, "I've got some bad news for you."

"It can't be all that bad," I said.

"Darryl," Jack said, "Jack Tatum's written a book."

"I heard something about it a few weeks ago on some radio show," I said. "Is it about me?"

"About you, about everyone." Jack said. "It's a sick book written by someone who must be sick."

"What's the book called?" I said.

"The title will sell a lot of books, Darryl," Jack said.

"So what is it?" I said.

"They Call Me Assassin," Jack said.

"No."

"Yes."

9 · A Slap in the Face

Jack Tatum. God, do I hate to hear the name Jack Tatum.

Let's forget, for a moment, the fact that it was Tatum who made the hit on the field in Oakland that left me in the condition I am today. Let's forget, for a moment, that the hit Tatum put on me was totally unnecessary and probably totally premeditated—both in the true Tatum tradition. What bothers me most about the man is that he had the audacity, and the insensitivity, to write a book touting that brand of football.

Jack Sands summed up Tatum's book for me over the phone: "Tatum describes in lurid detail how he coldbloodedly stalks NFL players and tries to KO them with such tactics as 'the hook,' which in Tatum's own words is the manner in which he conceals his elbow and then comes around and hits his opponent on the back of the neck—on the side that's blind to the official."

"I got hit by Tatum's hook," I interrupted, "and I know first-hand what it feels like. What's Tatum say about the play where I got hit?"

"He writes, and I quote: 'I could have gone for the interception,

201

but I went for the hit because that's what my owners pay me to do.' "

Maybe some owners do pay their players for 'hits,' but if they do, they should be booted out of the game. There is a wide line between a 'hit' as Tatum meant it, and a 'hit' as the great majority of NFL players mean it. A hit can be a clean hit. It doesn't have to be overly vicious. Tatum never understood that.

"Jack," I said to Sands, "does Tatum anywhere in his book express any remorse for what happened?"

"Are you kidding?" he said. "Throughout the whole book he gloats about all the players he's KO'd and sent to the sidelines limping or flat-out intimidated. I'll read you some more excerpts, if you can take it."

"Go ahead," I said. "I'm ready for anything."

"Page ten: 'Any fool knows that when you hit someone with your best shot and he is still able to think, then you're not a hitter. My idea of a good hit is when the victim wakes up on the sidelines with train whistles blowing in his head and wondering who he is and what ran over him.' "

I've had a lot of time to think about this remark of Tatum's, and all his other statements about how he happened to play the game. I played for a lot of head coaches and a lot of assistant coaches, and I read the rule books, and never—never, never, never—did I read anywhere that a 'good hit is when the victim wakes up on the sidelines with train whistles blowing in his head. . . .' Once again, maybe some NFL coaches and some NFL teams believe that Tatum's definition is the correct definition of a 'good hit,' but I never thought that way, and I know that most NFL players would never think that way. As Tatum made quite clear, he was out to hurt people. Nowhere in the rule book does it say that you're supposed to do that.

"Page eleven: 'I never make a tackle just to bring someone down. I want to punish the man I'm going after and I want him to know that it's going to hurt every time he comes my way.' "

Whatever you say, Jack. But what rule book did you go by? The NFL rule book? Or the Jack Tatum rule book? Nowhere in the NFL rule book does it talk about "never making a tackle just to bring someone down . . . and punishing the man . . . and wanting him to know that it's going to hurt every time he comes my way. . . ." But I'm sure that all those things were right there on page one in the Tatum Rule Book.

"Page eleven: 'I like to believe that my best hits border on felonious assault, but at the same time everything I do is by the rule book.' "

"That's all a crock of b.s.," I said to Jack Sands. "Fact is, Tatum had his own rule book and played by it."

"We all know that, Darryl," Jack said. "But there's more."

"Pages fifteen and sixteen: 'The Hook is simply flexing your biceps and trying to catch the receiver's head in the joint between the forearm and upper arm. It's like hitting with the biceps by using a head-lock type action. The purpose of the Hook is to strip the receiver of the ball, his helmet, his head, and his courage. Of course, you only use the hook in full-speed contact, and usually from the blind side.' " Ahh, there. He said it himself " . . . usually from the blind side." That was always the way Tatum got in his best licks . . . from the blind side. The best football players, in my opinion, were always front and center and head-on. Not guys who came at you from the blind side. I keep sounding like a broken record, but that type of football stinks. That's not how football is supposed to be played.

"Page seventeen: 'During a game at Denver's Mile High Stadium, I leveled the best shot of my career against Riley [Odoms].' Page eighteen: 'When I felt I could zero in on Riley's head at the same time the ball arrived in his hands, I moved. It was a perfectly timed hit, and I used my Hook on his head. Because of the momentum built up by the angles and speed of both Riley and myself, it was the best hit of my career. I heard Riley scream on impact and felt his body go limp. He landed flat on his back, and the ball came to rest on his chest for a completion, but Riley's eyes rolled back in his head and he wasn't breathing. I had another knockout, and maybe this time, I had even killed a man. God knew that I didn't want something like that to happen.' "

"Jack," I said to Sands, "Tatum's sicker than I thought." The fact that Odoms caught the ball *despite* what Tatum did to him didn't really matter to Tatum. The fact that Odoms was KO'd, though, was something Tatum took great pride in. Jack Tatum had another knockout. Most NFL players don't like it when one of their tackles knocks the wind out of another player, but Jack Tatum loved it.

"There's more to come," Sands said. "Catch this. Page twenty-one: 'During my second year George Atkinson suggested that he and I start a contest for who would get the most knockouts over the course of a season. It sounded like a good idea, and we agreed on a set of rules. First of all, neither of us wanted to get penalties called against us so we agreed that our hits must be clean shots and legal. Next, the man you hit would have to be down for an official injury time-out and he had to be helped off the field. That would be considered a "knockout" and it was worth two points. Sometimes, one of us would hit a man and he'd take the injury time-out but would limp off the field under his own power. We called that a "limp-off" and it was worth one point. When the season started, so did we. Actually, it was all part of our job, but we made a game of it. Guess who won?' " How can Tatum say that scoring a "limp-off" was part of his job? You get paid to make tackles and blocks, to score touchdowns, to kick field goals and extra points . . . to help a team win. You don't get paid for "limp-offs"—or at least we didn't.

"Jack," I said, "the guy who won was a real loser, in my mind."

"There's more, Darryl. Hold on. Pages twenty-six to -seven: 'My collision with Lynn Swann was, I admit, premeditated. I saw him coming across the middle for a pass, and even though Terry Bradshaw had thrown the ball in a different direction, Swann was still a fair and legal target. I don't want Lynn Swann or anyone in my area trying to catch passes. Most receivers know I earn my money and reputation with devastating hits. I don't care, but when the receiver operates as the primary target, I'm going to make him pay the price.' "

Right you are again, Jack. And I want you to know that I, Darryl Stingley, am paying the price every day, every single day. I'd like you to think about that sometime, when you reread your book and think about how you played the game of football. I'd like you to think about that when you recall the hit you put on me that night in Oakland—and what it did to me. Just think about that, Jack. If you do, I don't think you'll be able to sleep too well.

"Pages one hundred seventy-one to -two: 'My hit on Sammy White may well be the best ever in the history of the Super Bowl. It was one of those collisions that defensive people dream about and offensive people have nightmares over. Both Sammy and I were moving full speed and it was head on. During the impact White's helmet flew ten yards down the field, his chin strap shot twenty feet into the air, and some lady sitting near [Oakland Managing Partner] Al Davis screamed, "Oh, my God! He lost his head."

" 'Sammy was on the ground moaning for his Mama while I stood over him and issued another warning about coming into my area and getting hurt. I knew that Sammy was in no condition to hear my voice but his teammates were. That type of devastating hit has a tendency to discourage other receivers and running backs from trying anything over our middle. I had just wasted Sammy White. It—' "

"Hold it," I said to Jack. "Did Tatum say he *wasted* Sammy White?"

"Yep, those are his exact words, Darryl."

"I can't believe any pro football player would talk like that," I said. "Then again, Jack Tatum's not just any pro football player, is he? He calls himself Assassin. I don't know any other pro football player who ever called himself Assassin, or could ever look at himself in the mirror and say, 'I'm an assassin.' Yep, Jack Tatum is in a little world all of his own."

"Let me finish," Jack said. " '—it was a knockout, and believe me, it slowed the Vikings down. When his teammates gathered around, I could hear Sammy ask, Check my eyes! Are they still in my head? I can't see . . .' "

Finally, Jack said, "Darryl, here's exactly what he says about you: 'On a typical passing play, Darryl ran a rather dangerous pattern across the middle of our zone defense. It was one of those pass plays where I could not possibly have intercepted, so because of what the owners expect of me when they give me my paycheck, I automatically reacted to the situation by going for an intimidating hit.' "

"Whew," I said, "he sure said a whole mouthful."

"Darryl," Jack said, "the guy is really sick, no question about it."

"Jack," I said, "we've got to do something. If what Tatum said in that book is accurate, and if it's the way he plays the game, then the rules must be changed before the hospitals become filled. I don't see how he can be allowed to stay in the NFL. I want you to call Pete Rozelle and tell him that as commissioner of the NFL, as the man responsible for preserving the integrity of the game, he should ban Jack Tatum for life as a totally reprehensible human being who does not play the game according to the rules. Tell Rozelle that I'd like to talk to him myself, if he can spare the time."

Sands was furious, too. He was convinced, as was I, that Tatum had gone out of his way to hit me. He also was convinced, as I was, that the referee closest to the action had frozen on the play; there could be no other explanation for his failure to call a personal foul penalty against Tatum.

After Jack read me those excerpts from Tatum's book, I said to him, "Too bad I can't sue Tatum right now for the injuries he gave me in Oakland."

"You know what's really sad about all this, Darryl?" Jack said. "There's no doubt in my mind that when Tatum sat down and worked with his ghostwriter, he knew he was off the hook legally as far as you were concerned."

"Yeah, I suppose so," I said. "And this time he went for that part of me he didn't get before."

"Well put," Jack said. He added that calling Pete Rozelle was a waste of time, that whenever he called Rozelle the commissioner was always "in a meeting" and that the best thing we could do was write to him.

So on January 10, 1980, we wrote a letter to Rozelle in which we reminded him of some of the more inflammatory statements Tatum had made in his book; informed him that Tatum not only had not denied his published statements but had in fact repeated them over and over in the press; and asked that he immediately suspend Tatum indefinitely because his conduct struck at the foundation of the integrity of the game. By allowing Tatum to continue his style of play, Rozelle would seriously erode all public confidence in football.

It was a hard letter, to the point, and very necessary.

I thought that Rozelle would at least give us the courtesy of a quick and honest reply, either by phone or by letter. He had been quoted as saying that "Tatum was asking for it" in writing a book like *They Call Me Assassin,* and I thought he definitely would take some strong action against the man. To this very day we have not heard a word from Rozelle about Tatum's sick book, and not had any response to our letter.

We wrote again, and we even called, but still . . . nothing from Rozelle. One of the NFL's attorneys did write to Jack Sands, more than two months after the book hit the streets, and suggested that we'd be hearing from Rozelle in the future but that for now the commissioner was up to his ears with the Oakland Raiders' suit and a lot of other problems. What about my problems, Pete?

But what really bothered Jack and me was an assertion by an

NFL lawyer, Jay Moyer, counsel to the commissioner, that a longer passage of time between our letter to Rozelle and his ultimate response would serve some good in that it would allow both sides to look at Tatum's book more objectively. Or, as he put it in a letter to Jack Sands, "The passage of some time . . . is not without advantage; it should permit consideration of the matter and shape various reactions to that consideration on a more objective basis than would have been practically possible amid the emotional atmosphere generated by the book's initial publicity."

More objective? Look at me, Pete! I am a victim of a man proud to call himself an "assassin." Don't talk to me about being objective. If you want to develop some objectivity about Tatum, Pete, then consider me—and my quadriplegia. Also, Pete, I still have not heard your so-called ultimate response. I haven't heard a word from you. Not one.

Billy Sullivan told Jack Sands that the reason Rozelle failed to respond to our letter is that we used the press by sending a copy of our letter to various newspaper people. Did Jack and I ever laugh when we heard that. No one has ever used the press better than Pete Rozelle. Why, Pete Rozelle's initials are P.R.—as in public relations.

To the best of my knowledge, Rozelle never had Tatum on the carpet in his New York office or even discussed the contents of the book with him. That was my second slap in the face. The first was when Tatum made money on his book. In my opinion, the book wouldn't have sold without the notoriety he achieved from my injury spurring sales. Think of it: Jack Tatum not only gave me a broken neck and left me a quadriplegic, he also came back to give me a couple of slaps in the face for emphasis.

Nice guy.

There certainly were no tears shed around the Stingley household one morning just before the start of the 1981 season, when I read in a Chicago paper that the Houston Oilers had released veteran free safety Jack Tatum, whom they had acquired from the

Oakland Raiders the year before. Now that Tatum is out of football, the NFL is a better—and certainly safer—place.

Still there is too much of a violent air surrounding NFL football.
In the old days, the Dick Butkeses and the Alex Karrases played a
tough, dominating, physical game, but they never tried to hurt or
maim a player. They played football the way it was meant to be
played.

Not so with too many of today's players. They *are* out to hurt
people, to maim them, just like Jack Tatum did to me, and send
them to the hospital. And it's all part of a new and accepted NFL
society that operates not on the rules of the old society—"It's not
whether you win or lose but how you play the game"—but on the
new law of the football jungle—"It's not how you play the game
but whether you win or lose."

To the Jack Tatums of the NFL, putting a Darryl Stingley or a
Riley Odoms or a Sammy White out of commission for however
long is a worthwhile objective because it enhances their own
team's chances for victory and reduces the opposition's. Mind
you, I'm not about to suggest that the NFL suddenly become the
National Touch Football League. But the atmosphere of premeditated violence that now dominates the game—particularly in
the minds of the defensive players and the defensive coaches—
must change right now, or the NFL will need its own private
hospital just to care for all the players who'll need long-term
attention for their cracked skulls and broken necks and battered
bodies.

It is very diffcult for an offensive player to think or act with any
premediated violence, since his job is to avoid the defense. For
instance, as a wide receiver, my only thought was to try to read the
future moves of a defensive back; I'd run at him on four or five
plays and try to figure out the kind of move I could work against
him to break free and, ultimately, score.

On the other hand, the defensive player's violence is always
targeted. How is he going to stop that offensive player, intimidate

him, break up the play, knock the ball away? The nature of the game calls for defensive players to hit their opponents, grab their facemasks, twist their ankles, bruise their bodies, pile on, rap them out of bounds needlessly—anything to bring them down, inflict pain, and intimidate.

Call it violence. Call it intimidation.Call it intimidating violence. But it is there. It becomes an acquired skill, too, and it becomes incorporated into a team's game plan. Certain teams become known for it—but not all. When you think of the Dallas Cowboys, for instance, you probably think of Tom Landry and his precise attention to detail or his low-key exterior. When you think of the Pittsburgh Steelers, maybe you think of the brilliant offense and Terry Bradshaw throwing bombs to Lynn Swann. But when you think of the Oakland Raiders, the first thing that comes to mind is their roughhouse tactics on defense. The Oakland Raiders have always played the game with a certain style of mayhem that, in my opinion, is above the spirit of the rule book. And they've always gotten away with it. I'd like to know why.

Trouble is, the owners are making a nice buck for themselves by allowing violence to be such a major part of the game—and as far as I know they're not about to change anything that is boffo at that box office. Let's face it, the fans gladly pay admission for one reason: They want to watch football gladiators beat each other over the head at the coliseum each weekend. They love every minute of it. What the fans want is blood and guts, and more blood and guts. The more the merrier. So, the NFL owners keep giving the audience what it wants and keep stashing greenbacks in the bank.

Blood and guts sells. No question about it. And I'm not going to change that. Not me. Not ten Darryl Stingleys confined to wheelchairs. I can write books about violence in the NFL or go on television and speak out about it, as I have. I can propound solutions to violence until I'm blue in the face. But I'm just a grain of sand on the beach as far as the NFL owners are concerned.

There's no way they're going to put a lid on their money-making machine. No way. They'd rather pay the hospital bills.

Which is exactly what the New York Giants had to do on Thanksgiving Day, 1982, when Leon Bright, their ace punt re-turner, got hammered by Leonard Thompson of the Detroit Lions while waiting to catch a punt. Bright rarely calls for a fair catch, but according to the rules, the defensive player must give the punt return man enough room to catch the ball. I was watching this game on TV, and while Bright was waiting for the ball to come down, Thompson charged full-speed into him and laid Bright out cold with a forearm crack to his head.

My heart practically stopped when I saw Leon slump to the ground motionless for what seemed like a very long time. The Giants' doctors and trainers surrounded Bright, and I knew what was going through their minds—and probably through Bright's mind, too: Would Leon Bright be another Darryl Stingley?

After a while Bright began to show some signs of movement, and was taken off the field on a stretcher, transferred to an ambulance and rushed to the hospital. As it turned out, he had suffered a severe concussion, and his neck hurt. Some days later he was released from the hospital.

The whole country had seen Thompson's devastating hit on Bright because the Giants–Lions game was televised nationally. The next day newspapers were filled with stories blasting Thomp-son for his tactics, and the sports columnists all called on Pete Rozelle to take strong action against Thompson in an attempt to control what they called "the violent atmosphere of the game."

For three days, though, Rozelle did nothing, saying, as always, that he had to wait for a study of the films.

While he was studying the films, or his staff was studying the films for him, there was another violent incident right in Rozelle's backyard. In a game between Green Bay and the New York Jets at Shea Stadium, Jets linebacker Stan Blinka viciously hit wide receiver J.J. Jefferson of the Packers with a blindside forearm to the neck and head, KO'ing him for the count. To their credit, even the hometown fans booed the hometown player, and after the game Green Bay Coach Bart Starr strongly condemned Blinka's action. Jefferson later regained consciousness, but he was unable to play the rest of the game.

The next day, and for several days after that, the New York papers were filled with stories about violence in the NFL, and again the columnists urged Rozelle to step in and take a stand on violence, not ignore it as always.

In fact, the Thompson and Blinka hits probably were no worse than a lot of other cheap shot hits made in every NFL game, but in these two instances involved New York teams and, as a result, drew national media coverage because that city is the media center of pro sports. This time Rozelle really had no choice: he'd have to do something to keep the press off his back. He also needed some good press, too, since he had come out second best to arch-enemy Al Davis in the Raiders' courtroom victory that enabled the team to move from Oakland to Los Angeles, and since Rozelle had not been a significant figure in the long players' strike during the 1982 season.

So, Pete Rozelle acted. He fined Thompson all of $1000 but did not add a suspension, and he suspended Blinka for one game without pay (approximately $4500). When I heard of his actions, I just shook my head. Both Thompson and Blinka, I thought, deserved heavier penalties. Rozelle had the perfect opportunity to strike out against the violence that pervades this game, but he blew it. What he did was give those two players a slap on the wrist. Let me tell you something about fines. Players never pay fines; their teams pay the fines for them.

What Rozelle should have done was come down heavily on both Thompson and Blinka. Maybe he should have suspended them for the rest of the season—four or five games. Maybe he should have fined their respective teams—big, big bucks. What Pete Rozelle should have done, but what Pete Rozelle failed to do, was get the message across that the NFL will not tolerate violence of any kind, that players who want to play by their own rules, the rules of the jungle and the cheap shot, have no place in the NFL.

It was the perfect opportunity. And it passed.

To me, the solution to this pervasive violent atmosphere is relatively simple: All the officials on the field have to do is enforce the rules of the game. There's a rule book that the players are supposed to observe as they play the game. In reality, however, if a foul happens away from the play, away from the movement of the football, the officials will almost always overlook it. No harm done, no foul . . . that seems to be their attitude. But it's on just such innocent-looking plays that most of the cheap shots occur. I know.

Also, NFL officials all seem to operate with different standards —different notions of where to draw the line between acceptable plays and fouls. The officials meet for hours before each game to review the calls they made the previous week and study other films, but they never develop standards. For instance, a few years ago the NFL put in some new rules designed to better protect the quarterbacks. Well, the officials all call this rule differently. On the highlight shows on Sunday, you can see a quarterback on Channel 4 throw a touchdown pass with a defensive end all over him and have it count, and then switch to Channel 7 and see another quarterback throw a touchdown pass with a defensive end all over him—and have it called back and be declared a sack. There's no consistency among officials. None. I don't understand it.

Or maybe I do. The bottom line is that nothing will change until the fans start to squawk about it, until they stop buying their $20 tickets and stop turning on their television sets to watch NFL games. And that's not going to happen soon. Football has become a great social phenomenon—the tailgate parties, the Monday night drunken orgies, the long Sunday afternoons spent in front of the tube. To all these people, violence is just another issue of our time that's diminished in importance because everyone's gotten used to it.

But let me make one thing perfectly clear: I, Darryl Stingley, am a living example of what happens when violence is allowed to dominate a game. And if Pete Rozelle wants to do something positive for the game (usually his idea of doing something positive for it is directly related to achieving bigger profits for the owners) he can reverse this trend toward violence by having the officials read the rule book and enforce that rule book—to the letter.

I was not able to walk away from the game of football. I had to be carried. And that shouldn't happen to any player. I was afraid just such a thing was going to happen to my old Purdue roommate, Otis Armstrong, but he proved to be one step ahead of everyone else. Otis accompanied me to the 1980 Super Bowl game in Los Angeles, and for eight days we had adjoining rooms. He helped feed me, helped me drink out of a straw, helped me get dressed, helped me in and out of the door, helped me into and out of elevators, helped me into and out of my van. He did everything for me.

On the way back to Chicago, he said to me, "Darryl, I've seen what it's like to be dependent on someone for almost everything. I don't know how you handle it. I don't think I could ever do it."

Well, Otis had taken a helmet in the back during a game and at the time of our trip to L.A. he was experiencing severe neck pains. Doctors ultimately told Otis that his spinal cord is too large for his spinal canal. "One hit in the wrong place, just one hit," they said, "and you could wind up paralyzed for the rest of your life."

Soon after that Otis came by my place and we got around to discussing his injury. He said he was worried about his health, and thinking about retiring.

"Do what you want to do," I told him, "but really think about it."

I told Otis—even though he knew it already—that it wasn't

worth the risk for him to play anymore. He had had a great seven years with Denver. He had played in the Pro Bowl and the Super Bowl.

"One good hit or one good cheap shot, it doesn't matter," I said to him. "You've got your legs and your arms, and your life. That's all that matters."

Midway through the 1980 season Otis Armstrong suddenly announced his retirement, and when asked what helped make the decision for him, he said: "Darryl Stingley. Seeing Darryl, and knowing Darryl, made all this a lot easier. I want to walk away from the game of football. I don't want to be carried away from it."

10 · I'll Keep on Truckin'

Today, I weigh 156 pounds, about twenty-five pounds short of my old playing weight, and I'm ready to take on all comers in a wheelchair body building contest.

People always ask me, "Darryl, how do you manage to live in the condition you're in?" To me, there's only one answer: God. I've got to give credit where credit is due: He has kept me alive, and He is the reason I refuse to give up, that I refuse to press the switch forward on my chair and drive it through a window or down a flight of stairs. If that sounds like it comes directly from the storybook, I'm sorry—but it's true.

As kids, we had to write essays in school about what we wanted to be when we grew up. I'd always write about wanting to be a sports figure. I wanted to excel in sports. That desire was so strong that athletics came very easy to me, almost naturally. Now, God has presented an adverse situation to me—some would call it real misfortune—and, as I see it, my condition represents the ultimate test. The alternative is simple: death. No thanks. Instead, I thank Him for letting me participate in athletics for as long as I

217

did, and for my being a successful athlete. Thanks to sports, Darryl Stingley knows all about Darryl Stingley. Thanks to athletics . . . and to Him.

I am, you might say, a medical phenom. You know, to this day nobody has ever really explained to me what my condition really is. I've heard about it, mostly second-hand, and I've read about it over and over, but I don't really know exactly what it is. I guess I've been kept in the dark on a lot of things.

I'm not supposed to be able to feel anything from my neck down. Maybe I don't, but I know I *think* I feel everything from my head to my toes—and the doctors and nurses and therapists all tell me that such a constant thought is encouraging. The doctors in Oakland told my family that they didn't expect me to live through the night when my lung collapsed and pneumonia set in, but I proved them all wrong. The doctors in Oakland and Chicago have said that I'll never walk again, but if I have anything to do about it, I'm going to prove the experts wrong one more time.

What I really don't understand is this: If I'm not supposed to be able to move anything from my neck to my toes, why is it that I've been able to develop a pretty good range of motion with my right arm? When I checked into the Rehab Intitute in the fall of 1978, you remember, a therapist detected a slight movement in that right arm and was able to devise the switch system by which I operate my wheelchair. At the time it was all I could do to move that right hand onto the switch and manipulate it into the various positions.

By the early fall of 1982 my right-arm movement had improved so dramatically that I was able to throw out the first pitch at a Milwaukee Brewers game. Mind you, I didn't do an imitation of Don Sutton or Nolan Ryan and whip a high, hard fastball; in fact, I was more like Phil Niekro and threw a flutter ball. But I was able to lift my arm and throw the ball, if only for a few feet, and that represented an enormous achievement for someone who four years earlier could move that same arm barely an inch.

Overall, my condition has been described to me as extended state of shock, the result of that sudden and unexpected hit on the football field in Oakland. I'm a great optimist, as you've gathered, and I've convinced myself that maybe, just maybe, another great shock will occur and jolt me back into my old state. It could be anything. A car crash. A ride down the stairwell in my chair. A fall from my bed. A crack on the head when I'm in the bathtub. I don't know of anyone who ever thought something good might come from an automobile crash, but in my case, well, it just might.

Shock works in funny ways. At home one day my mother came into my room and gave me the bad news that a relative had died, and suddenly I was sitting up in bed. Incredibly, I went from a prone position to a sitting position—all by myself. It was strictly a reflex movement, something I had never done before—and something I've not done since that day. My mother couldn't believe her eyes.

"How'd you get sittin' up like that?" she asked.

"I sat up myself," I said.

"But you're not supposed to be able to do that by yourself," she said, shaking her head.

At other times friends have told me that they suddenly saw me do something like move my left hand, pick up a piece of paper with my right hand, or turn my right knee. I have, through physical exercise, developed my right arm and hand to the point where I have a good range of motion. But all the movements my friends detected are things that a quadriplegic simply isn't supposed to be able to do. Apparently, I made those movements, though I didn't realize it at the time. Again, they were the result of unconscious reflex reaction and were not planned acts. They all provide food for my hope, which is that someday I'll walk again.

I'm no doctor, but here's my analysis of Darryl Stingley's condition today, part by part.

My head feels fine. No damage up there.

My neck is twice as strong now as it was when I came out of the operating room in Oakland. I do neck exercises religiously, moving my neck up and down and side to side to strengthen the various muscles. Mind you, my neck's not the size of John Hannah's who wears about a size 20 shirt collar, but it's no longer the size of a straw, either.

My right arm was practically useless for the first year of my quadriplegia; I could just move my hand enough to operate the switch on my battery-powered chair. Today, I can raise that right arm over my head, and the dexterity of the fingers on my right hand improves each day. I still can't catch a perfect spiral, and I can't really reach out and grab things, but when you put something in my hand, I won't drop it. Come to think of it, the Patriot coaches always said I had good hands.

My left arm is a zero. In 1974 I broke that arm in two places while playing against the New York Jets, and I had to wear a cast for two months. My entire left side, the devil's side, as they say, has not responded to therapy in any positive way. In fact, it's always aching. Then again, the fact that I feel such pain is encouraging to me and my doctors. It's a sign that there's a reason to hope. If I didn't feel any pain, I'd probably be a celery stick.

My friends say they have seen me move my left hand, but as far as I know it has moved once, and only once, since I went down in Oakland. One day my sister Andrea was blow-drying my hair and the phone rang. Andrea put the dryer down and walked off to answer the phone. The dryer was right alongside my left hand and it kept blowing hot air against the hand. Suddenly, the left hand jumped. It was shocked into action. The fact that I haven't been able to move that hand in any way since then probably means that what happened with the hair dryer was a false alarm, but there's no getting away from the fact that the left hand did move—once.

I can feel my diaphragm expanding and collapsing. My lung capacity is not what it should be, because of my bouts with pneumonia every few months during the winter. But I work each day to develop my lungs. I practice holding my breath, and I use a machine that enables me to suck air in and hold it in for a long time before releasing it.

My legs certainly aren't active, but I occasionally have involuntary spasms in them—and, God, do they hurt. At night, when I'm alone, I try to wiggle my feet around, but I haven't had any success yet. People tell me that once I get something going, I should jump on it. When I try to wiggle my feet, I just try to get something going. I have great hope. Someday I *will* get something going. With His help, of course.

As for sex, all I can say is that, yes, I do have erections. One day I told my doctors at the Rehab Institute, "Guys, I'm ready to make another baby." That sure shook them up.

So far, everything I've done physically, or therapeutically, has been done according to my various doctors' orders, and with the advance approval of my insurance carriers. While I more than appreciate the technological advances being made in medicine, I have refused to experiment with any of the so-called miracle drugs. I also have been, and will continue to be, leery of trying some of the cure-alls people recommended to me in their letters.

A chiropractor wrote me and asked if he could crack my back, or my neck—or both.

"I guarantee you that my treatment will work for you," he promised.

Thanks, but no thanks.

I suppose there are a lot of people who'd like to be responsible for raising me out of my chair, for getting me to take my next step. For now, though, I'm sticking to what my doctors tell me to do.

As you might guess, I take a fair amount of medication each day, but none of it is what the doctors call "harsh." They've assured me that I won't get hooked on any of the drugs that have been prescribed for my regular use. Mainly, the drugs I take are designed to fight bacteria and prevent infection. I take 500 milligrams of vitamin C four times a day. I take a drug called Datrium, which is a mild relaxant to control involuntary muscle spasms;

those spasms, by the way, have been violent on occasion. I also take one Valium in the morning and another at dinnertime. And I take plenty of vitamin E, too.

These days I live pretty much by myself, though I'm not all alone very often. My mother moved out of my apartment in the summer of 1982 and moved in with my brother Wayne. I moved into my condominium on Lake Michigan in the summer of 1983 and life there is beautiful. The condo was designed expressly for me. If I had to describe my living situation there in a single word, I'd call it: *pushbutton*.

Everything I want is only a button away, or a few feet away in my chair. My secretary, Cheryl Gouldsby, comes by each day to help me keep up on personal matters, and I get regular visits from a physical therapist. And at night my pad is always alive with the sounds of my friends.

My dream, of course, is that someday soon Tina and the boys will walk through the front door and be back for good. I've come to understand, and accept, a lot of things about Tina. I know I really love her. I now understand all the things she did that turned me bitter. Particularly walking out on me. She just wasn't prepared or equipped emotionally to deal with me in my new state. (This was a problem for many of my friends and relatives, too.) What we've got to do, and are doing, is narrow the gaps between us little by little. It won't be long, I pray, before Tina and the boys, Hank and Derek, will be back living with me again. God, do I ever miss them.

Basically, I live in my battery-powered wheelchair, my Medi-Cline. When I first came home from the Rehab Institute, my nurses and family tried to get me to spend part of each day in a La-Z-Boy reclining chair in the living room of my apartment. I stopped that because I couldn't move around at all and felt as though I was in prison.

Wherever I go, my Hoyer lift machine goes with me. Whether I'm in bed, in my chair, or in a tub for bathing or therapy, I'm always on a white-mesh net with hooks that connect to the Hoyer machine. When it comes time for me to be moved, all someone has to do is connect those hooks to the Hoyer and press a button. The machine hydraulically lifts me from one position to another. It can drop me into bed, the chair, a tub, anything. My friends all call my Hoyer lift "Air Stingley."

I'm also hooked to a catheter, connected to my penis. Psychologically speaking, it's a godsend. One of my great fears is that someone will forget to reconnect my catheter, or connect it the wrong way, and I'll urinate on myself. When I was in the hospital in California and in the Rehab Institute in Chicago, I urinated on myself regularly because I could not control my bladder. I still can't control it, of course. Now, when I urinate, the flow is directed into a bag, which can be emptied without any problem by anyone.

I sleep late, very late, most every day. When I was on a rigid medical schedule at home and nurses were with me around the clock to give me therapy and medicine, I would get up at 7:30 A.M. and adhere to a strict daily regimen. Now I don't wake until just before noon each day but I still put in at least two hours of therapy, and take care of my business affairs, each day.

Most people start their mornings by getting up, moving about, scrubbing and shaving, and all that. Not me. When I get up, I don't really get up. The Hoyer just lifts me out of my bed and drops me into my chair. I'm up, but I'm down—unable to move about in any real way. Once awake, I'm bathed by my nurse. I used to be shaved every morning, but I got tired of people shaving me, so now I have a beard most of the time. Not a big bushy thing, just a good growth. My hair is sponge-washed every three or four days, and once a week I go to the barber shop for a shampoo, a facial, and a trim. My barber, Cleve Washington, is a good friend and my unofficial psychiatrist. We rap about a lot of things that I can't talk about with people in my family. When I leave Cleve's place, I'm always on a high.

I never was much of a connoisseur of food. At Purdue, and later with the Patriots, I was really a junk-food king. "Two all-beef patties special sauce lettuce cheese pickles onion on a sesame-seed bun" was my idea of The Pump Room. A couple of burgers, some large fries, a thick shake—a four-star meal. The New England coaches were always on me to eat three squares a day, but I never had the time, or the inclination, to prepare or even eat that many meals every day. No breakfast. Junk food at lunch. Junk food at dinner. A couple of beers and maybe some pizza at night. Who needed steak or veal à la Suisse?

Nowadays my breakfast consists of one simple item: a banana. In mid-afternoon I have some hot soup or a sandwich, maybe even both—something light with plenty of nutritional value. My most important, and biggest, meal is dinner, when, by doctor's orders, I have a very well-balanced menu. I eat steak most every night, along with salad, mixed vegetables, potatoes, then some ice cream or fruit for dessert. Later, before going to bed, I like to have a couple of beers—two at the most—because they put me in a restful mood.

When I'm just sitting around my apartment, I like to get into music. Music has always been a relaxing outlet for me. I have at least 3,000 albums and who knows how many tapes in my condo. When I'm in a bad mood, some good music will pull me out of it. I'm mainly an avant-garde mainstream jazz man. I don't buy the new disco. Miles Davis, John Coltrane, Les McCann, Chick Corea . . . they're my main men. When I close my eyes, I like the places they take me to. They communicate with sounds and voices in an intriguing way. Their music provides me with an escape from reality, which in my case oftentimes can be an ugly place.

If there's nothing better to do I watch television. For a long time I couldn't stand the afternoon soaps. Hell, my life was a real-life soap in itself so why should I watch more of them? Now I'm addicted to them—I watch 'em all. I don't mind a good cowboy movie, and of course I watch all the football and basketball games that are on. One thing I've discovered is that sometimes the best way to watch a TV football game is to keep the picture on but turn off the sound and listen to music instead. Football then becomes a whole different game, and definitely more enjoyable.

Mind you, I'm not some old stay-at-home stick-in-the-mud. No sir. I like to get into the van and get out and around with my friends, just like in the old days. I was pretty much of a night crawler when I had my legs and my Mark IV Continental wheels, and I still like life after dark—only I can't take as much of it.

It's never been a problem finding friends to go out with me at night. If there's a good NBA game down at Chicago Stadium (which isn't far from where I live) we'll take it in. The police around the stadium all know me, and they let me park the van right on Madison Street, alongside Gate 3. The Bulls have been very generous about leaving tickets for me and my friends, and I always sit in a favorite little spot on the floor, along the walkway that the visiting team takes to and from the court. In fact, the whole city of Chicago has opened its heart to me—and it's been a fantastic boost.

At least one night a week I try to get to a nightclub to hear some music, and if one of my favorite entertainers happens to be playing Chicago, you can be sure that I'll be there. One thing I'll never forget is the night I met Stevie Wonder, who'd always been an idol of mine, because of his music and also because he had overcome his own disability—blindness—to become such a smashing success.

People magazine was doing a story on me when Stevie came to Chicago, and the *People* writer said he'd arrange for me to meet Stevie after the concert. Here was someone I could relate to. My favorite song in the world probably was Stevie's "Higher Ground." I listened to those words every day when I did my exercise.

The concert was spectacular, just as I expected it to be. After Stevie finished singing, he came down and sat next to me and we talked—one disabled guy talking to another. It was fantastic! We

225

were alone; no one was within twenty-five feet of us. *People* photographers kept shooting pictures. So did my brother Wayne. I remember thinking to myself, "This is what it must be like when the President of the United States and the President of the Soviet Union get together for a private summit conference." After a half hour or so, Stevie had to go, but before he left he took an album cover I had brought with me and wrote the following inscription: "When things happen to people bad, like happened to you and I, lots of people think it's a bad thing, but this is not so. We're just part of God's army, and our purpose on earth now is to make people strong. We shall succeed." He initialed it "S.W."

Stevie sure set the record straight about what my real purpose in life had become, now that I was no longer a football player. He was a doer and I would become a doer, too. He was the most positive of people, despite his blindness, and I decided that I'd become much more positive than I'd been. My visit with Stevie was an overwhelming emotional experience for me, and typical of the way I've been treated since my accident. In fact, some friends of mine like to say that I've become "Chicago's guest." To say I appreciate this city and its people is an understatement. People have been great to me and I'd be hard pressed to tell them all how much it's meant to me.

If the weather's not too cold in the fall, I'm always the guest of George (Papa Bear) Halas for the Bears' games, with a seat right down there on the field, just where I always was in the good old days. The Papa Bear and I have become good friends. He writes me every so often and phones a couple of times a year, just to cheer me up. He's a very concerned, very sincere man. He even came to my surprise twenty-ninth birthday party at the Penthouse of the Conrad Hilton Hotel. The Papa Bear was more than eighty years old himself, but he was still the life of the party.

My travels have hardly been confined to the Chicago area. I've been to the Super Bowl in Los Angeles and Detroit; I was a member of Vice-President George Bush's private party for the

1982 Super Bowl at the Silverdome in Pontiac, Michigan. I flew on the Concorde to London, England, to accept the 1980 International Valor in Sports award. I went to Tulsa to be honored as one of the Ten Outstanding Young Men of America for 1981. I've flown around the country to do TV shows with Mike Douglas, Merv Griffin and for CBS's "60 Minutes." I went out on the road to meet Dick Gregory, who put me on a vitamin supplement and gave me a juicer and a lot of bags of grapes and stuff. I flew to Philadelphia and was driven out to Deer Lake, Pennsylvania, to be the special guest of Muhammad Ali while he was training to fight Larry Holmes.

"Hey, Darryl, you get in here with me and I'll whup ya good," The Champ kept saying.

"Not me, Muhammad, not me. I'm no match for you. The only way I could hurt you is to run you over."

"Just gimme that chair, Darryl. Gimme it. I'll ride it into the ring with me when I fight that Holmes and I'll run *him* over."

Until my trip to Deer Lake, I knew only the public Ali; I thought he was a loudmouth. In private, I found him to be humble, quiet, and shy—the exact opposite of his public image.

And, of course, I've made many trips to New England, not only to see the Patriots play but also to perform my role as the team's executive director of player personnel. I've sat in with the brass on the college draft, and I've looked at some game films for the coaches. I expect to do more for the Patriots in the future, as my condition continues to improve and I'm able to get around better. I enjoy my trips to Boston in every way. For as long as I'm there I stuff myself with lobster—lobster salad, baked stuffed lobster, lobster newburg, lobster bisque, you name it.

My trips to Boston also give me an opportunity to spend time with old friends like Jack Sands and his associate, Steve Freyer, whose constant prodding helped me get this book written before the twenty-first century.

I used to like to go to the Red Sox games, but I had a big

argument with a Yankee fan in 1980 and haven't been back to Fenway Park since. What happened was this: The ushers parked me in the aisleway behind home plate, and this big fat guy in a Yankee shirt and a Yankee hat kept standing up and wouldn't sit down.

"Down in front, down in front," I kept saying.

"Shut up, you bleeper bleeper bleeper," the Yankee lover said. "Why don't you make me sit down."

I laughed. But I want to tell you, the guys I was with sure made that Yankee lover sit down—and fast. One of the ushers knew me pretty well, and he told the Yankee lover that if he opened his mouth again, they'd remove him from the park—bodily.

My globetrotting aside, what I do most of the time, eight or ten hours a day, at least, is think. Think about Darryl Stingley. Who he is. What he is. Why he is. You know, it took an accident for me to know myself, to be content with myself.

My advice to people who find themselves in the predicament in which I found myself in 1978—a man suddenly deprived of his legs, his arms, his everything—is to be straight and honest with yourself about the realities of life. You can always wish for the best and have hope and faith in large quantities, but you can't escape grim reality. By being this way—totally honest—you'll put things in the proper perspective and leave them there, with the hope, of course, that someday maybe they will change. But since they're probably not going to change soon, do everything possible to make the best of your present situation.

Right after the accident I could have died, but I didn't. Now I'm left here in my chair, a quadriplegic. Who knows what the next transformation in my life will be? Or when it will come?

I've been able to cope because of the countless friendships that have presented themselves to me, and those I have developed on my own. Life really is no more frustrating for me than it is for other people who have physical problems or, worse, emotional problems. In fact, my problems may be less. Maybe I can't get around.

Then again, maybe by not being able to get around I've spared myself a whole lot of other problems. The NFL became infested with drugs in the mid and late 1970s and early 1980s. Who knows, maybe I'd have turned into a cocaine head, as did so many other players, including some who were good friends in my days with the Patriots.

There are certain things in life that I still strive for, and always will. As a matter of fact, I feel I have more things to look forward to than the average person. I'm definitely anticipating that day when I take my first step—my next step. I'm probably the only person who thinks it will ever happen, but just the thought of taking that step is enough to keep me going.

I'm also looking forward to that first controlled movement in my fingers—and really watching them move.

Taking a step, moving fingers—sure they're trivial things that most people simply take for granted. Not me. The thought of doing both helps make me happy each day and definitely stimulates me. No pain, no gain, that's what the therapists back at the Rehab Institute always told me. I'm gaining, but it's been a painful time all the while.

I know what my life was like before the accident, when I could walk around, run, dance, play football, do everything I wanted, whenever I wanted. So you can see why it's fun for me to think about being reborn physically. I try to look at life as a picture painted in a wholly different way: I think of myself as being special. Honest, it's not that hard for me to cope with quadriplegia.

In a situation like mine, you tend to get philosophical. You place reality right there in front of you, too, because you can't ever escape it. It almost haunts you. But you must have the wisdom to reason with yourself, and be strong enough to accept a condition that you are really helpless to change, and have the courage to keep going, to surge forward. When you think about it, it's the only alternative.

In a spiritual sense, I think I've been blessed by God. I don't

229

mind being His tool. I see myself as being an example. There's a whole new purpose to my life: I'm not a wide receiver, I'm His example. I can make statements to people that will help sustain their lives. I can tell them, and show them, that there's always an outlet.

There's always hope when you get to the end of your rope. Just tie a knot and hold on. I'm holding on, and I'm living.

I think how every day my life will get better. And it has, every day, every single day, from the first day of the accident—zero point—when I was one step from the promised land, to today. I was given a second chance in life, and I've watched myself grow and grow. I've improved so much that at times I'm not even aware of it. I still look forward to having more peace of mind regarding my family life, and to a greater acceptance of my situation by others. I don't have many other goals. I'm not a football player, so I don't look forward to being All-Pro. I just hope that through my happiness I'll be able to help someone else be just as happy as I am.

When people tell me, as they have, that I'm an inspiration, well, it brings me to tears. I can help people more, do more for people, in my present condition than I could when I was a football player. When I'm gone, when He calls me, I'd like to be remembered not as the football player who had an accident, but as a man who made a great contribution to his fellow man.

Maybe that all sounds corny, but it's how I feel. Being so close to death so many times has taught me a few other realities about life, or a few other ways of looking at life. I don't go for all the gusto. I try to move through life with a definite purpose. I look at myself as a spiritual person, because I know I can't be a physical person anymore. So, what I'm trying to do is cultivate that spiritual side, make it grow. It would be easy for me to feel sorry for myself, but that thought has never even entered my mind. At the hospital in California when I got around to thinking about the future, I asked Him, "Why me?" and came up with the answer right away. I realized, of course, that God is a loving God and wouldn't want to bring harm to me. The way I saw it, He allowed the accident to happen in order to make me see something or realize something. He picked me out. He chose me so I could learn that which I had to learn in order to be a better person.

Thanks to my God, I feel I'm a somebody. I'm not just a former NFL player. I can be an inspiration to my fellow man. There is no reason for me to feel that He has punished me in any way. Because I had such a life-threatening experience, I can see death now almost as a friend, a friend that allows me to get more out of life. I'm here to carry on as long as I can, to touch as many lives as I can. When he has finished using me for those purposes, maybe I'll be lucky enough to get up and out of this chair on my own. He's the one who gave me another chance and every day I thank Him for it. I don't worry about anything now. I just sit back and count my blessings.

I'm happy to be alive.

Epilogue

Yes, I'm alive, but I had another close call—another brush with death—on the night of February 1, 1983, almost exactly four and a half years after my accident on the football field in Oakland.

Around dinnertime I was alone in my apartment, in bed relaxing, watching the six o'clock news on TV and talking on the telephone to the interior decorator about the decor for my new condominium on Lake Michigan. Suddenly, I heard an explosion, followed by loud voices, and then a whole lot of screaming everywhere. I didn't know what the hell was happening, just that something wasn't right, and that I'd better take care of myself—or else.

"What's wrong, Darryl?" the decorator asked. "What was that big boom I just heard?"

"Don't know," I said. "But call my sister and tell her I need her right away."

I gave him Andrea's number and hung up. Andrea had lived in my apartment building until a few weeks before, when she moved a couple of buildings away. I knew she was home, and that she'd get to my place quicker than quick.

I still had no idea what was happening, but I was scared because I could hear people screaming. I called a friend of mine in the building, Willie Little, an old high school teammate who was the assistant basketball coach at the University of Illinois's Chicago Circle branch. Willie wasn't home, but his brother-in-law, Glenn Franklin, was.

"Glenn, it's Darryl. Something's going on up here, and I think I need help. Can you come?"

"Darryl, I'll be right there."

My apartment was on the eleventh floor, a few floors above Willie's, and thank God the door wasn't locked.

Glenn arrived in a flash, and when he came charging through the door, a whole lot of smoke came in with him. In no time at all, my apartment was filled with it. Glenn had never been in such a situation before. Dealing with a quad, or anyone, for that matter, at such a time, requires a cool head, and Glenn had just that.

He opened a window so we could breathe some fresh air and the smoke could filter through the apartment. I looked over at my television set, but the smoke was so dense I couldn't even see the screen. And there was bedlam everywhere, with people screaming and glass breaking and sirens shrieking.

"Glenn, get me out of bed, will you?" I said.

"I can't see you, Darryl, where are you?"

"Over here, over here, over here . . ."

"I'm coming."

At the time he was screaming out the window to the people on the ground, "Hey, I've got a quad up here—I need help—somebody, please help me."

"Darryl," Glenn said, "they're sending up a ladder for you."

"No ladder for me," I said. "How can I go down a ladder?"

I was taking short, panting breaths, trying to keep the smoke out of my lungs but not succeeding. Racing through my mind as I lay there in bed—helpless—was the same thought I had that night in the hospital in California: It's all over for Darryl Stingley. I'm checking out. "Darryl," I said to myself, "you made it through once, but this probably is it."

Just then a couple of firemen came through the door with their big flashlights and found Glenn and me in my room.

"He's a quad," Glenn said to the firemen.

"I'm a quad," I said, struggling to breathe.

The firemen were in total control. They wanted to lift me out of bed and carry me downstairs.

"No," I said. "It'll be better if you put me in the wheelchair and push me out of here. The chair's right over there." One of the firemen got the chair, and Glen and another fireman lifted me out of the bed and into the chair. I wasn't settled the way I normally was, but I wasn't about to complain. They wheeled me through the apartment and out the door, then down the hall and out onto the fire escape. That fire landing was like heaven. Fresh air. Oh, did that feel good.

The two firemen then lifted my chair and carried me down the fire escape to the tenth floor. It was a cold trip. All I was wearing were my briefs and my support hose. Then Glenn found a blanket and wrapped it around me. Once we reached the tenth floor, they wheeled me back inside, down the corridor to the elevator, and then into the elevator for a fast trip down to safety.

When I was wheeled off the elevator and out into the lobby of the building, I was greeted with a hug and a kiss from Andrea and with loud cheers from a few dozen other people. It was a real victory celebration. Then a team of paramedics arrived and wheeled me to an ambulance, where they gave me oxygen. Those guys were really alert. They asked me what medication I was taking, who my doctor was, all the right questions. I wasn't worried about a thing. Not anymore.

All this time Glenn was by my side; I owe my life to him. Glenn went with me in the ambulance down to St. Luke's Presbyterian

Hospital. The paramedics just wanted the doctors to give me the once-over, and I was all for it, too. My whole family—my father, my mother, my two brothers, Andrea, everyone—arrived at the hospital within an hour and a half, and we had a great reunion. The doctors released me, and it was agreed that I'd go to Andrea's apartment for at least the rest of the night. But before we could escape the hospital, the press—newspapers, TV, radio—arrived in full force.

"I'm just happy to be alive," I kept telling them. "Just happy to be alive."

I didn't know the details of the fire until the next morning. Apparently a guy had had a fight or a falling out with his girl friend, and to get even he decided he'd set her apartment—with her in it—on fire. So he took a can of gasoline, rode up to the eleventh floor, and walked down to her apartment door, which was near the middle of the floor. He poured the gas all around her door, and then poured a trail of it all the way down the hallway to the elevator door, which happened to be opposite my own door. He pushed the button to get the elevator, and when it arrived he struck a match and ignited the gasoline. Then he was off, down the elevator to safety. In no time the hall was on fire, and there was an explosion when the fire reached the pool of gas around the door of his girl friend—his ex-girl friend, I guess. The thing was, she wasn't even home at the time; she had gone out for the night.

The tragedy was that two neighbors of mine—two young women, one in her thirties and the other in her twenties—were killed in the fire. When they heard the explosion and smelled the smoke, they opened the door of their own apartment and almost immediately became engulfed by the flames. I guess they panicked, because they ran back into their apartment, and as the flames continued to roar into their apartment, they opened the window and jumped out. They were killed in the fall.

A day or so later, the man who started the fire turned himself in to the Chicago police.

When the press reports of the fire were released in the papers the next day, one of the paramedics was quoted as saying, "It was unbelievable how calm Darryl remained throughout the whole ordeal." And one of the firemen was quoted as saying, "Darryl never showed any signs of panicking."

What was there to panic about? I had to be in control. I had to be able to tell people how to deal with me and my condition. And another thing. I had been there—near death—before. It was an either/or situation, just as in the hospital in California. I was either going to make it, or I was going to die. So it was nothing for me to become hysterical about.

I was not ready to die when I was in the hospital in California, and He wasn't ready to take me. I also wasn't ready to die the night the fire swept through the floor of my apartment building, and again He wasn't ready to take me. I had the will to survive, and I survived.

I don't know how many lives one person gets. I probably used up three of my lives in the hospital in 1978, and I probably used up another three the night of the fire. How many more do I have left? Only He knows.

What will be the climax to the story?

Only He knows that, too. And I'm in no hurry to find out.

237